Soulmates

Our journey with MSA

By John Gibbs

Published by JR & SC Gibbs Publishing

First published in 2021

A CIP catalogue record for this book is available from the British Library

ISBN (Paper)	978 1 8383529 0 5
ISBN (Electronic)	978 1 8383529 1 2

Typeset on Garamond 12pt

Printed and bound by Amazon and Kindle Direct Publishing

This book is dedicated to Sue,
all the other people with MSA,
family and friends impacted,
and the healthcare professionals and others
who are committed to improving
the lives of the terminally ill.

Chapters

Part II

Part III

Foreword

Multiple System Atrophy (MSA) is a rare, neurological disorder that affects adult men and women. It is caused by degeneration or atrophy of nerve cells in several areas of the brain and affects all of the body's basic functions – walking and balance, speech, swallowing and incontinence. Reading about Sue's experience of MSA sadly reiterates some of the most challenging aspects of it - a fast progression of the disease which quickly deteriorates to a reduced quality of life to the point that the affected individual will need 24/7 care.

Due to the rarity of MSA, many families feel lost when they get the life-changing diagnosis, and I am pleased to learn that John and Sue approached the MSA Trust for help. We are the UK's only charity supporting people living with MSA, their carers, family, and the relevant heath and care professionals. We have factsheets, our own magazine, an informative website and a supportive online forum. Our services include an email and telephone helpline through which MSA Nurse Specialists provide advice on symptom management. We run a network of local Support Groups across the country that enables people to meet others with the condition, so they no longer feel alone.

The first part of this book is a heart-warming account of John and his 'soulmate' Sue's journey that strikes a balance between the harsh realities of the illness, and most importantly the humour with which they faced this devastating condition. I hope you will find their approach to battling MSA as uplifting and motivating as I did, and John's retelling of their life story a fitting tribute for his wife.

The second part is a practical, self-help guide that describes the approaches the couple took to managing the symptoms of MSA. We are so grateful that John took the time to share the details of the various processes, equipment and care pathways that helped Suzanne. I would, though, like to take this opportunity to remind the reader that this is John and Sue's individual journey, and may not necessarily be everyone's experience of MSA. If you or someone you know has been affected by MSA, please contact the Trust or a medical practitioner before adopting any process or advice given in this book.

John has tirelessly initiated support for the Trust after losing Sue. Her tribute page alone has raised more than £10,000 in 2020 and came at a time when the fundraising was needed the most. He has also kindly decided to donate the proceeds from the sale of this book to the Trust, and we so are so thankful for the continuous fund and awareness raising.

Wishing John all the very best success with this book and any future endeavours,

Karen Walker, Chief Executive
MSA Trust

Part I

A peaceful end

Sue passed away peacefully with the sun shining through the window. She was pain-free, relaxed and comfortable. One of the carers was holding her hand, Jan our next door neighbour was holding her other hand, and I was in my usual place, at her feet.

It might seem strange starting our story here as multiple system atrophy (MSA) is, indeed, a cruel illness, however it is important that people realise the end can be a peaceful moment. Many MSA patients, and this was certainly the case for Sue, spend unnecessary hours worrying about how things will end.

Like most people with MSA we did not know that Sue had MSA at the start. She started off with strange symptoms that seemed to be random and disconnected: a series of urinary infections, acute pains in different places, holding her arm in a defensive position, a clenching of her fingers, a subtle twitch in her little finger, and louder snoring. We had several false starts in finding an answer. These were not the fault of anyone, it was just due to the complexity and rareness of MSA. It was only after MSA was suspected that these symptoms seemed to make sense.

Our journey with MSA made us stronger as a couple, reinforced my feelings for Sue repeatedly, and made me realise how lucky as I was to have had her in my life.

The start of our journey

Our wedding outside Dannah Farm, Shottle, Derbyshire

The start of our journey

Sue had not been blessed with the best of health. As a child she had glandular fever. Then, in her early twenties, she had Crohn's disease, a horrible illness. This meant Sue was unable to continue as a Primary school teacher even though the children, parents and teachers adored her – a common feeling for those who knew her. I could write a separate book on how we battled with Crohn's disease, her recovery from major bowel surgery and how we tried to live a normal life. During this time, I realised that my beautiful fiancée had an inner strength that surpassed that of anyone I have ever met.

Having come to manage Crohn's through a mixture of surgery, drugs and diet, we got married in September 1995.

Our wedding was a low-key affair as we were saving up for a deposit for our first house together. We got married in Ripley registry office (not the most attractive of venues). I remember the drive to our wedding. I was in the front of the car with Sue's grandmothers sat in the back. All they talked about was the Second World War and rationing. Perhaps with hindsight it was an omen of the battle that Sue and I would have with MSA.

The ceremony went more smoothly than the journey to the venue. Sue had written out vows based on a love letter from Victor Hugo in 1821...

When two souls,
which have sought each other for
however long in the throng,
have finally found each other
...a union fiery and pure as they themselves are...
begins on earth and continues forever in heaven...
This is the love which you inspire in me.

As newlyweds we headed for our wedding breakfast in a small country pub and had a lovely meal washed down with gooseberry champagne (it was cheaper than the real stuff, but my Mum hated it).

The pub had a goat in the garden, and she made an appearance in our wedding photos. Grandma pointed out that with Grandfather's wispy beard, it wasn't easy to tell one from the other.

Following a couple of nights in the "luxury spa retreat" we moved into our first house together, a new build on a new housing estate called Heatherton Village in Derby, Derbyshire. When we arrived, we discovered that the house had been broken into, but because there was nothing else there, the thieves had only stolen the toilet seats.

In 1998 Sue was dealt the blow of endometriosis, another cruel illness. Any woman who suffers from this will tell you of the monthly agony of her menstrual cycle. Too often Sue would be doubled over in pain and all I could do was hold her hand and tell her it would soon feel better. After many recurrences and surgeries, Sue was placed in a medically induced menopause to stop the endometriosis. This was a difficult decision for us at the time as we were effectively deciding not to have children but stopping the pain was worth the sacrifice and neither of us regretted that decision.

For what seemed like the first time in ages we had some normality in our lives as Sue, now in her late twenties, had her first period of stable health for a long time, but it was the calm before the storm.

Searching for an answer

January 2012 to May 2015

Sue with her Mum and Dad in Trafalgar Square, London
December 2014

Searching for an answer

January 2012 to May 2015

Out of the blue, and after five years of stable health, Sue started to have menstrual bleeding and excruciating pains. Endometriosis had returned, this time accompanied by ovarian cysts. Several endoscopic operations were performed – one of which did not go well resulting in an infection and some necrosis that needed to be resolved with a further procedure. We still do not know whether endometriosis was the first symptom of MSA or whether the urinary infections that she had over the previous 18 months were, however, it was the start of a long journey in search of an answer.

≈

With unbearable pain, and having now suffered multiple occurrences of endometriosis, Sue decided to have a full hysterectomy to stop the pain once and for all. On waking up from the operation she smiled at me and said that this was the start of the rest of our lives.

As Sue recovered from the operation, she had further abdominal pains that could not be explained. She had multiple scans, but nothing was conclusive. It was decided that the only course of action was pain management: tablets, injections and therapies.

Smiling throughout, but clearly in enormous discomfort, she tried to carry on. I think that this was probably the lowest point of our story. With chronic pain you just want to know that it is going to go away – it affects so much of your life. But Sue's inner strength shone through and she never complained (well only to me and when no one else was in ear shot).

During this time, she had more urinary tract infections (UTIs) and in the grand scheme of things these did not seem to be as important. We found out subsequently that repeated UTIs are the first symptom in over 50% of people with MSA.

With the pain getting worse we decided to seek further medical opinions and were referred to a nerve conduction specialist.

He performed some interesting tests, putting needles into Sue and trying to stimulate the nerves to see whether there was anything wrong with them. He could not find anything, but it was worth a shot. Apparently, me asking if I could turn the dial up on the power of the electrical stimulation was not very funny. (This was not the first, or last, time that inappropriate humour helped us on the journey.)

As the nerve conduction specialist was taking off the sensors, he noticed a slight twitch in Sue's finger and referred her to a neurologist.

Whilst all of this was going on, Sue was scouring the internet looking for an explanation for her symptoms. Nothing made sense.

By the time we saw the neurologist Sue's finger was moving independently slightly more. The neurologist sent Sue for a DaTSCAN which helps visualise dopamine transporter levels in the brain, an indicator for Parkinson's disease. The results were not good. There were significant dark areas on the scan, which showed her dopamine levels were almost non-existent.

An MRI scan was also performed and highlighted some abnormalities.

At the age of 42, Sue was diagnosed with the severe early onset of Parkinson's disease. I remember the consultant saying, "It could be worse." Back then we didn't realise what that meant but in time we were to find out.

We now had the name for Sue's illness and whilst there is no cure for Parkinson's disease, the symptoms can be improved, and the full onset of the illness can be delayed with life expectancy being "near to normal".

The consultant started Sue on the usual Parkinson's disease treatment, trying to restore the dopamine levels using medication such as Stalevo.

As the consultant rapidly increased the level of medication, we saw little, if any, improvements. In fact, things started to worsen.

Despite not having the Parkinson's disease shuffle that normally occurs much later in the illness, Sue started to fall over. The first three times we were able to make an excuse. She fell in the garden and we thought she had tripped over a step. The second time, she fell when having just stood up from a chair. The third time was when she got out of the car. Each time, thankfully, she did not really hurt herself although she did bruise her head.

In parallel Sue started to have problems sleeping. She was often restless, moving her arms and legs more than normal, and waking feeling tired in the morning.

The urinary infections continued with regularity. This triggered separate activity with urologists who, after taking bladder scans, were talking about urine retention as an issue.

We knew our consultant was concerned. He decided that Sue needed further scans and that we should see a specialist for more tests. Searching on the internet we realised that the specialist was focussed on an illness called ***multiple system atrophy***. This was the first time we had heard of this illness.

During the next month two different scans and tests highlighted the following:

- A Cardiac MIBG scan returned normal. This was not good: the Cardiac MIBG scan is abnormal in Parkinson's disease and usually normal for MSA patients.

- Autonomic tests were conducted including a tilt table. I must admit that I found these tests really intriguing. By lying on a table and tilting it, while sitting down, standing up, eating, walking, it measures how blood pressure reacts to different scenarios. Sue's blood pressure was not reacting in the way it should, swinging from very low to very high but not at the right times.

Further tests were required in London, so we decided to take Sue's parents with us and stay over the weekend which came as a welcome break from the stresses of the tests. Sue's

Dad is a massive Elvis Presley fan and there was an exhibition of Elvis memorabilia at the O2 arena. It included a lot of items from Memphis. Sue and her Mum didn't fancy the exhibition, so I accompanied Sue's Dad. He enjoyed it so much we returned from Derby the following weekend for a second break to London. This time all four of us went to the exhibition.

We also visited the National Gallery as Sue loved her art. Her favourite painting was "The Hay Wain" by John Constable so we looked at that painting for what seemed, to me, like a very long time. It wasn't just paintings Sue loved, but also modern artwork with her favourite sculptor being Antony Gormley (more about that later).

As reward for my patience we visited my favourite UK museum, the Natural History Museum.

Having completed all the tests, we returned to see the consultant. Sitting in the room and armed with the results he broke the terrible news. Sue had MSA-P, with the P denoting that the predominant symptoms were Parkinsonian.

Finally, we had the answer. But it was the one that we never wanted to hear. Less than twelve months earlier, we had sat in the same room thinking it was early onset Parkinson's disease. We were devastated with that diagnosis, realising that our lives would never be the same. Now we were being told that Sue's life expectancy was much shorter, perhaps six to ten years from first onset of symptoms.

Looking back, it is obvious now that the consultant suspected MSA all along but was hoping Sue would respond to the treatment. Realising she was not; he had tried to break the diagnosis to us gently.

≈

There is no definitive test for MSA; diagnosis is based on clinical observations and indicative tests. There are other illnesses that have similar symptoms and test results. As the illness progressed there were a couple of times when the symptoms that presented themselves were out of line with the norm and I found myself asking or challenging the diagnosis (knowing in my heart of hearts that it was MSA but hoping for a miracle that it might be something else). The reality, of course, is that most of the other options had similar outcomes anyway.

At times of crisis and uncertainty we all need answers, especially when faced with the terminal illness of the most important person in our life. It certainly triggered a million questions for me.

Sue's and my responses were very different, and neither of them were right or wrong, though when I look back through our 25 years of marriage, I realise that Sue was always right, and I was nearly always in the wrong.

For Sue, having the name of the illness was the most important thing. She had been searching for years to understand what all the different symptoms meant. Hours had been spent online looking at illnesses, with Sue often asking me whether it could be X or Y. Her searching stopped as soon as we had the label of MSA. She felt at last that people would understand that she had not been imagining or exaggerating the symptoms. She knew that the illness was terminal but was not interested in reading about it. But she was not putting her head in the sand. She was getting ready for the battle ahead and was prepared to face whatever MSA would throw at us.

I was different. I had done as much searching as Sue and now I had a name I was going to understand everything there was to know about this illness. I had so many questions. I read everything I could find and it was scary. I then did what I should have done from the start and turned to the UK's MSA Trust (a charity set up in the memory of Sarah Matheson who was diagnosed with MSA in 1993). I had my first phone call with one of their nurses. She was amazing. She showed patience as I went through all my questions, answering where she could, reassuring me where she could not.

I was really looking for the answers to two questions. Both were impossible to answer:

1. How long has Sue got?

2. What is going to happen?

The official answer to the first question is that the life expectancy of someone with MSA-P is somewhere between six and ten years from onset of the first symptom, which is not always clear. It also depends on the person's age, the state of their health, the progression rate, and so on. It is the proverbial: how long is a piece of string?

The second question is equally important. You want to prepare for the illness and know what is going to happen. That is challenging as different people get different symptoms and the severity varies considerably.

≈

The first challenge we faced was telling others that Sue had MSA. I found these conversations difficult. I broke down in tears several times as I told our parents, siblings, friends and my colleagues at work that Sue had a critical illness. We do not have children, so we were saved that difficult conversation, at least. The reactions from people varied wildly from shock, horror, sympathy, tears and even being matter of fact.

MSA is a rare illness affecting approximately 44 people per million. That equates to about 3,000 in the UK with most being over 50 years old and fewer than 400 below. Most medical professionals will not come across this illness in their career and thankfully nor do most of us. But the rareness triggered one common question: "What is MSA?" It is not an easy question when you are still coming to terms with the diagnosis, you do not really understand the illness and how it is going to progress, and your emotions are all over the place.

The UK National Health Service describes it as:

> "…a rare condition of the nervous system that causes gradual damage to nerve cells in the brain….
>
> …affects balance, movement and the autonomic nervous system, which controls several basic functions, such as breathing, digestion and bladder control…
>
> …symptoms usually start between 50 and 60 years of age but can begin at any time after 30."

The rareness made me struggle with one particular question: "Why Sue?" At the time of writing, this question is impossible to answer as there is no known cause of MSA. There are many options being investigated.

One line of thought is the accumulation of a protein called alpha-synuclein as it appears to be more prevalent in people with MSA. Other avenues being explored include a possible inheritance or environmental factor but there is no evidence to support these hypotheses.

I realise that life is not always fair, but I do believe that things happen for a reason. I was put on this earth to look after Sue and make sure she had the best life possible. I think that she suffered with MSA so that we could learn and help others.

≈

It's at this point I should introduce Jan into the story. She has been the most amazing neighbour.

We had only moved into our house a few years before Sue started to have symptoms. As we searched for an answer Jan stepped in and regularly took Sue out for lunch to keep her spirits raised. I was envious of those "ladies at lunch" sessions as I sat in the staff canteen eating bland cheese sandwiches.

I call Jan our "angel next door". She gave so much of her time to help us and she features in so many of the happy times during our journey.

Afternoon tea at the Ritz

June 2015 to early October 2015

Sue with my Mum, Dad and me having afternoon tea at the Ritz Hotel, London to celebrate Mum and Dad's 50th wedding anniversary

Afternoon tea at the Ritz

June 2015 to early October 2015

The progression of Sue's MSA was like playing a game of whack-a-mole on a roller coaster. The illness would progress with new symptoms appearing at random and us trying anything to minimise the impact on the quality of her life. And we were doing this with all the emotional highs and lows, and twists and turns that a terminal illness throws at you.

Sometimes the illness would progress quickly and sometimes there would be periods of stability.

By the time that Sue was diagnosed in May 2015 her symptoms were mild. I use that term carefully as this is relative. With respect to MSA and what was then to come, mild is the right term, but most people would describe the symptoms she had then as significant.

≈

We applied for Personal Independence Payment (PIP). I had to complete the 40-page DWP application form as Sue's writing had deteriorated.

The form asked questions that we expected and were easy to answer such as Sue's condition, medication, and treatment.

Other questions were more difficult as it forced us to really understand how the illness was already impacting us such as preparing food, eating and drinking, dressing and undressing, communicating, reading, and washing and bathing.

We also had to talk about some very personal topics such as toileting needs, before we had even come to terms with it ourselves.

Discussing this made us realise that things had changed significantly, and they were going to change even further.

I was surprised about the breadth of the questions as it also covered other topics which we had not even considered, such as Sue's ability to mix with other people, make decisions about money, going out, moving around, and anything else that might be relevant.

The form is daunting.

My advice is to make a note of all the things that happen over a two to four-week period as it is difficult to remember everything. It is worth doing this accurately and completely as the payment can help with some of the changes you will need to make and bring in additional help.

The process is also time consuming. From the time we applied, through to submitting the form, having an interview and the final notification of approval, the whole process took three and a half months.

≈

By the time the PIP was approved in June Sue was still walking but now needed a walking stick or pole to aid balance. Thankfully she had stopped falling over but was worried that she might freeze or fall when she went out. When standing it looked as though she was slightly slouched, and her head was now stretching forwards and down. Her smile, still warm and disarming, had a droop to it. Her voice was getting quieter.

Her two little fingers on her left hand were clenched tight. She was now struggling to prepare food and was having difficulty cutting it as she could not hold a normal knife or fork. We bought large handled cutlery in order for her to hold it more easily.

Her diet had changed, and she was eating food that was easier to handle. It made eating slow.

She found it difficult to sleep and was tired all the time. She had even fallen asleep eating a couple of times. Her snoring seemed to be getting louder. She slept better on her side but was struggling to stay on it during the night. We purchased a triangular wedge side-positioning cushion that ran the length of her back and enabled her to sleep.

Sue was not able to get herself in or out of the bath; I would have to lift her. She couldn't wash her own hair. She struggled to dry herself and sometimes to dress herself. She was still able to go to the toilet but was starting to wear incontinence liners due to mild urinary incontinence.

≈

Still reeling from the diagnosis, we felt we wanted to have a short break to celebrate Sue's birthday, so we decided to head over to Guernsey. Sue and I had completely opposite philosophies on getting ready for holidays. She wanted to pack weeks in advance; I always wanted to pack at the last minute. Our flight was leaving early Sunday afternoon from East Midlands Airport so this time I won the battle and planned to pack in the morning.

I was woken by Sue at 7am. She felt a burning pain and it looked like she had another urinary tract infection (UTI). I phoned 111 and explained the situation. They told me to take Sue to the walk-in centre and we would be seen at 9am. After getting both of us dressed (as Sue now needed help dressing) we arrived at 8.45am with me reassuring Sue that we could still make the flight.

There was a queue of people who all thought they had a 9am appointment, and, more frustratingly, the GP had disappeared. I looked at my watch every five minutes until he reappeared at 10am (thankfully we were shown straight in).

I explained that Sue suffered from UTIs, that I had performed a UTI dipstick test, which was positive, and that we required some antibiotics. He was not buying it and wanted to go through the whole of Sue's history. Eventually at 10.30am he "diagnosed" a UTI and wrote a prescription.

The problem was that there was no pharmacy at the walk-in centre. "Don't panic,", I told Sue. "We'll still make the flight. We'll pick up the antibiotics on the way back home".

We got into the car and I phoned the chemist explaining the urgency and that I would be the lunatic running through the shop. To their credit they had it ready for me as I ran in and out at 11am.

As we raced home, I kept saying to Sue that "we can make it" referring to the rapidly nearing flight time. I was equally trying to convince myself.

I left Sue in the car as I ran into the house. Dragging out two suitcases I crammed Sue's things into the two cases adding some items for myself as good measure. Grabbing Sue's medication and stuffing it into a rucksack, I ran back to the car. I had packed in 15 minutes flat.

By now it was 11.30am – just 90 minutes until the flight was due to depart.

Accelerating towards the airport I phoned the car drop-off people and said we were running "slightly late" and that we would need "some help" when we arrived. Pulling into the car park they were ready with a buggy. We climbed aboard and were whisked through security, bag scanning and to the gate. We arrived at 12.15pm with 45 mins to spare. The gate had not even opened.

I proudly turned to Sue. "I told you we would be okay packing in the morning!" (I am not sure she agreed with me).

We had a great time in Guernsey, but I could see that Sue was struggling more and more with walking. We decided to go to the beach. She found it tough, but we were both determined that she would get the chance to dip her feet in the sea. Unfortunately, she just could not manage the distance.

At this point you would expect the gallant husband that I am to pick up my wife and carry her piggyback to the water. Instead, thankfully, one of the lifeguards (a very fit young man in shorts) who had seen us struggling drove over to us. Picking Sue up in his arms he took her down to the water, leaving me in his trail.

Learning from our outward journey I packed the night before. In reality it was mainly because Sue nagged me so much that I gave in.

We arrived in plenty of time at the airport only to find that the flights were delayed due to fog. Why is it that when you need a delay everything works fine, but when you are on time everything is delayed?

≈

In July Sue began to struggle walking up and down stairs. The effort was tiring, and I was very worried she might fall. However, she was determined to keep climbing the stairs. It was this determination that helped our battle with MSA, but it sometimes meant we had disagreements about what to do and when. It was only after a couple of "near misses" on the stairs that Sue finally agreed something needed to be done.

There are many options on the market that can fit any staircase situation, for example, the bottom of our staircase is next to the lounge door, so we needed a stairlift with a hinged bottom so it wouldn't block the doorway. We also needed one that could be controlled by someone else to cope with Sue losing dexterity in her hand. After looking at several options we ordered a stairlift and it was installed within a couple of weeks.

I did not realise the symbolism of the stairlift at first but once it was installed it was a constant reminder of the illness. It was the first thing we saw as we entered the house, every time I went up and down the stairs, and of course whenever Sue wanted to go up and down. Sue did not like it because she had decorated our house beautifully and it was now the very first thing that every visitor saw.

Despite this the stairlift really helped. It gave us both peace of mind that Sue was safe and meant she was able to continue to sleep upstairs with me.

When Sue eventually started sleeping downstairs, I could not bring myself to remove the stairlift as it felt like I was saying she would never sleep upstairs again. When she passed away it remained in place for many months because coronavirus restrictions prevented the company from entering the house. The stairlift remained a constant reminder of MSA throughout and after the journey and it felt an important moment when it was eventually removed, and I could restore the hallway to the way Sue had wanted it.

≈

Throughout May and June, it was clear that Sue was struggling, and we needed help, but both of us were in denial. We felt that we could continue as we were and did not want other people in the house.

The near misses on the stairs caused us to pause and reflect on the other areas that Sue was struggling with. We reread the Personal Independence Payment (PIP) form we had and realised that she had got worse over the interim period. Whilst it was not easy, we finally acknowledged that we needed help.

It turned out that the decision to have care was easier than choosing which care company to use, as there were so many to pick from. I spoke to our GP Care Coordinator and the MSA Trust to get their views on what to look for and the questions to ask. I also asked family and friends for recommendations.

We asked three companies to visit us and discuss our needs. Ahead of these visits we prepared a list of questions which I have included in the "Some hints and tips" section starting on page 185. These reflect our learnings as we engaged other care companies further along our journey and our experiences of care provision.

Having selected the care company, we sat down with their care coordinator to agree the care plan. As I was helping Sue get out of bed, washed and dressed, and then have breakfast she decided that she wanted help in the morning to reduce the pressure on me before work. We therefore arranged three visits (Monday, Wednesday and Friday) for an hour each.

On Monday 3rd August 2015 the first carer entered our lives. She was the first of over 110 daytime and night-time carers who helped us on our journey. It was her caring, understated style that meant the transition to having someone in the house was less traumatic than it might have been.

≈

Sue was struggling to sleep and feeling more tired. Our consultant suggested Sue went for an in-depth sleep analysis. In August we went to Addenbrooke's Hospital in Cambridge for the sleep trials. We chose Addenbrooke's as the consultant there had experience of sleep disorders for MSA patients.

Sue was admitted for an overnight test and was sitting on the bed when the consultant walked in (I was sitting in a chair). He said to Sue that it was unusual for someone of her sex, age and weight to be suffering from sleep apnoea as it was normally men of a certain age and weight who have the problem. He looked at me directly as he said that, I found myself sucking in my stomach and looking away.

A cap was put onto Sue's head with cables coming off and connected to the machine so they could do the EEG monitoring of her sleep patterns. I am sorry to say that I burst out laughing – she looked hilarious.

The results were in by the time I returned the following day. She had a sleep apnoea hypopnea index of 46. This meant that she had partial (or full) loss of breath for more than ten seconds over 46 times in an hour. A normal, healthy person would experience zero. Sue's score was classified as severe.

They also identified body movement when Sue was in the Rapid Eye Movement (REM) phase of sleep. Healthy individuals normally have vivid dreams accompanied by temporary muscle paralysis to protect them. Movement during REM sleep indicated a sleep behaviour disorder.

She had restless legs, heavy snoring, and screaming in her sleep. No wonder she was tired. They also said that my sleep was probably being affected as well, which wasn't much of a revelation to me.

The treatment was to put her onto an auto CPAP (continuous positive airway pressure) machine. This is a small machine with a lightweight, flexible pipe that is attached to a mask that fits over the mouth or nose which is then worn overnight. The machine then provides a pressurised airflow that kept her airways open to prevent blockages. She did not always find this comfortable, but it improved her sleep pattern slightly and left her less tired.

≈

It was my Mum and Dad's 50th wedding anniversary in October 2015. We decided to treat them to a weekend in London and afternoon tea at the Ritz. My sister and brother-in-law joined us for the trip.

Taking the train down to London we arrived at St Pancras train station and decided to have a cup of tea in one of the cafes on the platform. A brave pigeon flew onto the table and tried to eat my Mum's scone. It still makes me smile remembering Sue and my sister laughing at Mum's mortification.

Prior to the trip my sister had said she did not want to go to the Ritz, so my sister and brother-in-law decided to have lunch at the Hard Rock Cafe. Going our separate ways, we arrived at the Ritz all dressed up with my Dad complaining constantly about "how expensive it was for some cucumber sandwiches." I kept pointing out that he was not paying but secretly agreed with him. I think he would have preferred to be with my sister at the Hard Rock Cafe.

I must admit though that the afternoon tea was a great experience. Most importantly my Mum said it was amazing. She had always wanted to go there, and it lived up to everything she had hoped for. It certainly made up for the pigeon episode of the previous day.

Meeting back up with my sister we decided to continue our treat and went to Harrods. In the taxi Sue mentioned she was a bit tired so we agreed we would only stay for 30 minutes and then go back to the hotel.

The taxi pulled up outside. As we got out of the cab it was clear that Sue was struggling. In a way that can only be described as compassionate the doorman suggested to Sue that she used a wheelchair which he had available. This was the first time Sue had used one. I think she only agreed to it because it was a "Harrods wheelchair" – she did have a knack for spotting the best of things. We had a great time and were able to stay for a couple of hours. Even better, we did not buy anything.

It made us realise that we needed to start thinking about using a wheelchair more often so we could enjoy activities for longer. We wanted something that Sue could use to provide some stability, just to rest on, or use as a full wheelchair. Being the fashion icon, she also wanted something that looked good, so we settled on a Rollz Motion All-In-One Rollator & Wheelchair.

This was a big moment in the MSA journey as the increased use of a wheelchair is normally associated with progress of the illness and loss of independence. We viewed it differently. We saw it as liberating and a way of ensuring Sue could enjoy the activities we were doing.

This positive attitude really helped us fight MSA.

≈

In parallel to the Guernsey, Cambridge and London visits we started to have conversations about how we were going to cope as the MSA symptoms worsened. I am so pleased that we were proactive in this as the illness accelerated and we only just managed to stay ahead of it.

The most important decision we made was that we would care for Sue at home for as long as possible and ideally for the duration of the illness, which we managed to do.

It was clear though that our house was not suitable for someone who was going to need complex care. We decided to start modifications to the house so that Sue would be safe in the short term and well cared for in the longer term.

This is when Steve, our builder, entered our lives. He made the whole process bearable as we planned ahead and made some modifications to the house that would help us care for Sue at home.

A ramp was put up to the front door to make it wheelchair accessible and we widened the front door and some of the internal doors to make it easier to navigate through them.

The garage was converted into a bedroom and wet room for Sue to sleep and shower downstairs. We installed bi-fold doors to let in a lot of light and air. We put grab rails everywhere for Sue to hold onto when she moved around.

We replaced the carpets with hard floors so the mobile standing aid (which would be used to help Sue stand up and sit down) and hoist (which would be used to lift Sue in and out of bed) would be easy to move. Both of these devices are on wheels and it is easier to move them on hard floors compared to carpet.

Decking and a ramp were built in the back garden for Sue to enjoy the outdoors.

I built some raised flower beds using heavy wooden railway sleepers. Sue enjoyed watching me struggle with the weight and length of them, but the effort was worth it. With the flowers being at head height when she was sitting in the wheelchair, she was able to join in planting. This involved her pointing and telling me what to do. She was clearly management material.

As our home became a building site for several months Steve was brilliant with Sue as she constantly wanted to see what was happening. He would hold her hands and keep her steady as she moved around the rubble.

I also wanted to keep an eye on progress so one day I returned home early. Everything was quiet but I could hear laughter upstairs. As I climbed the stairs, I realised it was coming from the bedroom. The door was shut.

Unannounced I swung it open to find Steve in the bedroom with Sue and one of the carers. Thankfully they were all clothed and just stared at me. I think they were more shocked that I had finished work early.

By now Sue was also getting cramps in her feet and legs. Bizarrely (and I do not know how she discovered this) one of Steve's builders was a very good foot masseur so the building work slowed down as they spent more time massaging her feet than converting the house.

Eventually the work was completed. We would be able to live together in our home for the whole of her battle with MSA.

Once the building work was completed Sue then demonstrated her amazing sense of decor and made the whole house stunning. She could easily have had a career as an interior designer.

For example, she spotted a silver, grey and white wallpaper that had leopards and feathers in it. The unusual thing about this wallpaper is that the leopards and feathers change colour as you walk across the room. Even more interesting is that normally, when adults see it for the first time, they see feathers and miss the leopards. When children see the wallpaper, the opposite happens.

I was even more impressed that Sue had managed to find white decking that matched the white wood effect tiles in the bedroom and bathroom. It created a seamless flow from inside to the outside, especially when the bi-fold doors were open. Towards the end Sue loved to have these doors open wide as she was able to stay in her bed and let the garden come into her room.

A smashing time

mid October 2015

Sue in Duffield, Derbyshire
the weekend after a smashing time
mid-October 2015

A smashing time

mid-October 2015

Jan, our angel next door, was the neighbour that the carers relied on to help them when things got too difficult. Just a couple of weeks after the building work was completed, I returned home to find everyone in the kitchen. Sue and Jan were drinking sherry and the carers were ashen-faced drinking tea.

Sensing a problem, I asked what was wrong.

Unable to speak they pointed towards the newly finished wet room. As I walked into the room, I found glass everywhere. There must have been a million bits of glass covering every part of the floor except a beautifully clear path to the toilet.

The carers had taken Sue to the toilet. Once seated they had tried to close the wet room door. Instead of just sliding it, they managed to pull the door towards them. The 2.3m high x 1.5m wide glass door had dropped off the runner onto its end, shattering into millions of pieces. It had covered everything and everyone.

Panicking they ran next door to seek Jan's help. Entering the house Jan found Sue sitting on the toilet with glass everywhere including in her knickers.

Overcoming my initial annoyance at the scene I burst out laughing when imaging the scenario. It took me over five hours to clear the mess up.

The mile-high club

Late October 2015 to March 2016

Sue in Fira, the capital of Santorini, Greece
overlooking the Mediterranean Sea
Late-October 2015

The mile-high club

Late October 2015 to March 2016

For those of you who skipped the first few chapters and have gone straight to this one expecting to read something raunchy then I am sorry to let you down.

With the diagnosis, the sleep apnoea and the building work we felt we needed a real holiday. Knowing that this might be our last holiday together and having not had a proper holiday for several years we decided to treat ourselves with a cruise that started in Rome.

The trip to London had demonstrated to us the power of the wheelchair and its ability to allow Sue to conserve energy and therefore enjoy experiences more. I discovered that airports provide a free service for wheelchair users where you are greeted at the entrance to the airport and assisted onto the plane, therefore removing the hassle.

Upon checking into the hotel, I realised that I had left one of Sue's Parkinson's medications, a patch rather than tablets, at home. The hotel rang for a doctor and within 10 minutes one arrived. After getting a prescription, I went to the pharmacy. It was good news – they had some patches in stock, however the cost would be €700. This is when I discovered how lucky we are to have free prescriptions on the NHS. As I walked into the hotel reception having spent our total holiday funds, I was then greeted by a smiling receptionist holding an invoice for €100 for the doctor. No wonder he was fast.

We had a lovely time in Rome. It is such a beautiful city with friendly people. To conserve Sue's energy, we rode on tour buses or horse drawn carriages to see the sights. When walking she would use a stick or occasionally the wheelchair. When she needed a rest, we sat in a cafe people watching.

On the Monday we left Rome to travel to the Celebrity Reflection, our cruise ship and home for the next ten days. We were greeted by Maritza who would take personal care of us. She was amazing and made the trip so special. We weren't the only ones to think so: Tom Cruise had recruited her previously as his personal assistant. She supported him, travelling all over the world, but remained tight-lipped when I probed for juicy gossip.

We set sail and visited Santorini, Athens, Mykonos, Ephesus, Rhodes, Crete, and Naples before returning to Rome. In addition to waking up in a different location every day we took advantage of some of the other benefits of going on a cruise.

There were organised excursions suitable for less mobile guests, which involved less walking but still included all the sights. I think we managed to see more of Athens than most other people, but without the effort or the crowds. We visited a jeweller and watched them making necklaces. I bought one for Sue which she wore all the time. It is worth its weight in gold to me as it brings back so many memories.

Sometimes MSA comes to the rescue and that was the case in Santorini. As everyone else headed for the donkeys to ride up the steep hills we chose the cable car. Because of Sue's condition we were able to jump the queues and arrived at the top straight away. We watched as hundreds of people struggled to stay on the donkeys or queue for the cable car. It is always worth asking for help.

We went for a cabin mid-ship, so everything was close by. The crew were always willing to help, and nothing was too much effort. It is a shame I cannot say the same about the passengers. Most people were kind and considerate. Unfortunately, there were a small minority that were less considerate. They either just did not know how to interact with wheelchair users or live in their own worlds and do not realise their behaviour makes life more difficult for others. A simple example of kindness was just moving a chair when we were trying to weave through a restaurant. Do not be afraid to ask people if you need assistance.

We enjoyed dressing up each night and eating in the wide variety of restaurants on the ship with each one knowing our needs without having to ask. It felt so normal at a time when things were starting to be very different.

Flying home Sue decided she needed the toilet. Being unsteady on her feet and not helped by the movement of the plane, my assistance was needed. Walking backwards and holding her hands, I guided her to the loos where two cabin crew were talking nearby.

"My wife isn't very well," I explained to them "and she needs my help going to the toilet – I didn't want you to get any wrong ideas."

Quick as a flash the cabin crew member replied, "Don't worry sir, you don't look the type."

Feigning injury I retorted "I've never been so insulted in my life!" and then promptly slammed the door behind me.

In the confined space of a plane toilet Sue and I "crashed" and "banged" around for quite a while. We emerged from the toilet to find the crew member waiting for us. In a sheepish voice she apologised, probably taking into account my saying that Sue needed help and regretting that she had made a flippant remark that I could easily have complained about.

I burst out laughing "I have never heard anything so funny – I just can't believe I do not look the type!"

Returning to our seat Sue then asked me what the exchange had been about. "You know, the mile-high club," I replied. She asked, "What is that?".

Each time the crew member passed by our seats for the rest of the flight I kept saying to her, "I can't believe I don't look the type". Sue kept telling me to stop and that it was embarrassing. I still do not know what she was more embarrassed about. Was it me "not looking the type" or, by implication, that she did?

≈

We realised on holiday that Sue needed more help at home, and we would have to increase the level of care. As I couldn't afford to give up work to become a full-time carer, we needed more help from the carers, but this was expensive. Upon returning home we therefore started the challenging process of getting funding approved to help pay for some of the care. I say challenging for three reasons:

1. I discussed very personal information about Sue in a "matter of fact" way, which was emotionally difficult.

2. There is not enough money available to provide the care that every person needs, made worse by people who manipulate the system. As a result, those performing the assessment try and maximise the use of the limited funding available. I didn't take their push back personally and stayed focussed on putting a good case forward so we could get the funding in place to provide the right level of care as Sue's condition progressed.

3. Asking for help was not something I was used to doing. On the flip side I was demanding, persistent and resilient which are some of my strengths.

There are two major sources of funding available in England.

The first is Social Services. The process started by applying for a Social Services "Needs Assessment", which consisted of discussing the daily routine, how Sue struggled and what support she needed. The challenge with this route is that it is means tested. Even though you may not be entitled to funding it is worth pursuing. It registers the need for help and can unlock access to other resources and equipment. You may be assigned a dedicated social worker (I found Sue's social worker to be extremely helpful throughout Sue's illness).

The second route is NHS Continuing Healthcare, which is similar but focussed on Sue's health needs. This includes the complexity and intensity of the symptoms, how unpredictable they are, and risks to health if the correct care is not provided at the right time, e.g. the ability to take medication and impact if she was unable to.

After an initial application an assessment meeting was arranged, which involved different healthcare professionals including representation from our GP practice, social services and the care team. This Multi-Disciplinary Team (MDT) met regularly. The MDT ensured that everyone who was involved in Sue's care understood the current situation, which was especially important given that MSA is a rare and complex illness that changes continually.

Membership of the MDT changed over time as new specialities were needed. Whenever we saw a significant change in Sue's condition, I would request that the MDT meet at our house to decide on the next steps. This proved very effective in delivering the right level of care at the appropriate time.

The first challenge for a newly formed MDT is to use the Decision Support Tool to assess Sue's care needs. The assessment covers multiple domains: breathing, nutrition, continence, skin, mobility, communication, psychological and emotional, cognition, behaviour, medication, states of consciousness, and other significant care needs.

Each one is assessed on a six-level scale ranging from the lowest level of "no needs" to the highest of "priority". To secure funding required the domains to be classified with at-least one at the highest level, i.e. "priority" or two at the next level down, i.e. "severe".

Whilst it was clear that Sue needed help the criteria were so stringent that she did not qualify for funding. According to NHS guidelines there is some flexibility and funding may be provided if there is one severe and several other complex needs.

We had several meetings with the MDT where needs were revisited; part of the challenge of MSA is the rapid, progressive and unpredictable nature including life expectancy.

Over several months and many meetings, we were awarded a low level of funding, co-funded by both Social Services and the NHS Clinical Commissioning Group. Whilst this did not cover all the carer costs it certainly contributed. It is worth noting that our GP issued a DS1500 form that helped the discussion.

We agreed to more frequent reviews than the usual annual cycle. This enabled us to review Sue's care needs as the illness progressed and discuss any potential increases in care and funding.

There are other areas where financial help can be obtained. For example, we applied for an NHS Medical Exemption Certificate, which meant Sue received free prescriptions. Even though MSA does not feature on the list of qualifying medical conditions, you can still obtain one of these by discussing it with your GP.

≈

MSA is an interesting illness in that some of the symptoms are challenging to control. For example, in Sue's case she had already started using incontinence liners for urinary incontinence (the unintentional passing of urine), but these were no longer appropriate when her incontinence worsened in December 2015.

The normal options for treating urinary incontinence were not appropriate as she was also suffering from urine retention (the inability to fully empty the bladder). This led to urinary infections and courses of antibiotics.

We were referred to the Urology team. They gave Sue a device for stimulating the bladder to empty, thus reducing the threat of urinary infections, and advised Sue to start using incontinence pads which were provided by the Incontinence service. She was able to use these for around 18 months before having to swap to incontinence pants in April 2017. These are not available on the NHS but are far more effective.

Urinary symptoms were not the only symptom that varied wildly and made treatment more difficult. Her blood pressure would fluctuate from very low to very high and she would swing from diarrhoea to constipation. For the latter we used a bulk forming laxative or high fibre food. When that didn't work the district nurse would occasionally visit to give Sue a suppository.

≈

Sue was having more sleep disturbances towards the end of 2015. She seemed to be acting out her dreams which resulted in me being hit by a flailing arm several times. Oddly, her arms seemed more relaxed and flexible while she was asleep, and she had more movement.

There were two things that I found really cute. She would laugh during her sleep and her feet would move quickly up and down. It reminded me of Thumper in the Bambi movie. As the illness progressed, I would sit by her side watching her do this, wondering what she was dreaming about and wishing I could be part of it.

Sue still needed my help to get up and go to the loo during the night and those interruptions plus all the noise and movement including the CPAP machine meant I was no longer getting enough sleep.

We decided that I should sleep in the spare bedroom. In early 2016 I moved rooms. This was a major deal for me as I felt as though I was abandoning her.

She still needed my help to go to the loo in the night, however she could not shout loud enough to wake me up. The answer was an alarm with a buzzer that she could wear around her neck.

Every night at 2am and 4am she would press the buzzer. The alarm went off like a house alarm (it was that loud). There was also a bright white light that would strobe just in case I didn't hear it

Sue would sometimes just press it to check my response times. I think that I would have given Usain Bolt a run for his money.

A new set of wheels

April 2016 to September 2016

Sue and Jan celebrating
HM Queen Elizabeth's 90th birthday
June 2016

A new set of wheels

April 2016 to September 2016

MSA can affect the production and control of saliva which, alongside the postural issues that cause the head to lean forward, can result in the saliva pooling and running out of the mouth rather than being swallowed.

During the times when she had saliva around her mouth and chin, we would put lip balm or Vaseline on to protect her lips and used balm tissues to wipe the saliva away. These are much kinder to lips compared to using handkerchiefs, flannels or normal tissues (which might chafe) and more importantly no one wants a soggy handkerchief wiped across their chin continuously.

To help remove excess or thick saliva from Sue's mouth we initially used oral swabs (little sponges on sticks) that we would move gently around the sides of her mouth effectively pulling the saliva out manually.

As the illness progressed, we were given a suction machine that could remove more saliva from further back in her mouth.

In April the issue of saliva control worsened.

We were referred to a neurologist specialising in Botox injections. He explained that there are three main types of salivary gland that produce saliva to keep the mouth and other parts of the digestive system lubricated. The plan was to inject two of these: the parotid glands and the submandibular glands, with the aim of reducing the amount of saliva they produce. He was able to locate Sue's glands using his fingers and then injected Botox using a very fine needle. It was a very simple procedure.

The injections really helped the saliva control issue. Within about five days the saliva stopped leaving her mouth and running down her chin. It would usually last for three months, so we repeated this process every four months.

As the amount of Botox needed varies from person to person, he started off with a lower quantity on our first visit and then slowly increased it in subsequent sessions.

≈

Sue was now regularly using the wheelchair and was spending more time sitting in it. We needed something that was more comfortable, so it was time to call in the experts: the NHS Wheelchair Services team.

Getting the right wheelchair(s) is important. There are many options so, as with all our appointments, we prepared ahead. We listed the problems that Sue was having, what we were planning to do and how the wheelchair needed to support Sue's needs, and critically, how the wheelchair would support my needs too.

The last point may seem odd, but it needs to work for the person in the chair and the person who will be supporting them. For example, with MSA the person will not always be able to propel themselves manually so an attendant may be needed.

We ended up with three different wheelchairs being delivered. The first two were manual; the third was electric.

1. The first chair was an Invacare Action 3NG. This is great for putting in the car boot as it is light and foldable. For comfort we bought a pressure cushion to sit on and used this as the main wheelchair until mid-2017.

2. The second chair was an Invacare Rea Azalea. This is a sturdier wheelchair. The main advantage is that the seat and the back can both be tilted independently. The disadvantage is that you cannot fold it into a car boot.

   Sue found this chair a lot more comfortable as we could adjust the back and feet supports. We could also recline her which helped in three ways. It reduced the strain on her neck as her head was dropping forwards. Tilting her backwards meant she could look ahead easier. It also helped with the saliva control and pooling at the front of her mouth and on her chin.

   She always used this second chair in the house and started using it outside from mid-2017. We used this wheelchair until the end of our journey, and it was essential to us continuing to experience life together.

3. The third chair was an Invacare TDX SP2. This chair is electric, and a big advantage was that Sue could raise the seat so that the head is at the same height as someone standing up.

Before I go any further with wheelchairs, I should say something about Sue and cars. Sue did not really enjoy driving even though I told her she was a good driver. She did, though, have a few "interactions" with objects and other cars. I remember receiving a call at work. She had hit a petrol pump. I rushed to her aid. Rounding the corner, I expected to see a scene from Lethal Weapon with the car on fire and plumes of smoke rising. Thankfully she had hit the concrete plinth not the actual the pump. The car had come off worse with the wheel hanging off. Launching her defence, she said that the petrol pump had jumped out. She would often take the chance to remind me that she had passed her test on her first effort and I had taken five attempts.

You may be wondering why I would mention Sue's car driving at this time. Well, coming back to the electric wheelchair, neither of us realised that Sue would have to pass a test before they would allow her to take it out in public.

The wheelchair centre was close to a major roundabout and the test included driving on the pavement and crossing the roundabout at several places.

Not realising that there was a sensitivity setting for the rate of acceleration and speed which had been accidentally set to maximum, Sue shot off down the pavement with the Wheelchair Services clinician and me running after her. Weaving from side to side, we just managed to catch up as she got to the first pedestrian crossing.

Even after adjusting the settings, we realised that Sue was still struggling to keep control of the wheelchair. The outcome of the test for Sue was that she had failed but after a lot of debate and escalations we reached a compromise when I persuaded them that we would only use it in the house and that she would benefit massively from raising the seat.

In hindsight that may not have been the best compromise I have ever reached as the skirting boards, doors and other items in the house and garden still have the marks from side swipes as she navigated the house.

Given her driving of the wheelchair it is ironic that she hated dodgem cars at fairs.

≈

In June 2016 we joined our neighbours to celebrate Queen Elizabeth II's 90th birthday. The picture at the start of this chapter is Sue and Jan in one of our neighbour's gardens. They hosted a street party. It was a beautiful warm summer's day. We toasted the Queen with champagne and ate strawberries. One of my funny memories was pushing Sue's wheelchair down their gravel drive. I found out that wheelchairs and gravel are not the best of friends. Having struggled to push the wheelchair down the drive I turned around to see I had created two deep ruts in their otherwise neat and tidy drive. I found myself quickly pushing the gravel around to literally "cover our tracks".

Later that month we went to Whitby for the weekend and did not realise at the time that this would be our last holiday in a "normal" hotel. During the trip back we visited Bettys

Tea Shop in York, which was Sue's favourite place to have afternoon tea. We both loved their Blue Sapphire tea.

≈

In July 2016 Sue was struggling to get comfortable in a normal chair. She could not get up out of the chair on her own. Instead I, or a carer, would help her get up which was a challenge for everyone, so we bought a riser recliner chair. The riser function was to help us as much as Sue. The recliner function meant that we could tilt her backwards. This helped in different ways. It eased the aches and pains in her back, legs and arms. Just like the second wheelchair, it also helped take the pressure off her neck and head.

We met with a physiotherapist to discuss how we could get Sue even more comfortable. Our thoughts were to purchase inflatable cushions and other items, but she told us a different solution that cost nothing and allowed us to get Sue comfortable irrespective of whether she was sitting or lying down.

By simply using a combination of soft cushions and rolled up towels we were able to support Sue's hands, arms, legs and feet so that the pressure was taken off them. As her illness progressed her feet dropped and again rolled up towels helped mitigate the aches and pains.

When we went out, I had to manually transfer Sue from the wheelchair into the car. I would lift Sue out of the wheelchair, swing her through 90 degrees, "drop" her into the car, lift her legs, rotate her in the car seat and then straighten her up. It was not ladylike in any way and strained my back.

To get her out of the car was the same in reverse. I searched online and found a rotating seat cushion that could sit on the car seat and help me with the rotation, but the whole procedure was a real challenge.

≈

In September 2016 Sue was struggling to get comfortable in bed. She could sleep on her side but could not get her legs right and would fall back onto her back. She could not adjust her own position easily. She also preferred to sleep with her head slightly raised as this helped the saliva control.

Following advice from the occupational therapist we switched our normal bed for a four-way profiling bed. This is a bed where different sections of the bed that support the head, back, bottom, legs, and knees can be adjusted independently to help with posture and to assist the carers in various tasks such as moving and handling. The bed was supplied by the NHS and they also delivered two mattresses, one was foam and the other was an air mattress.

Sue found this change difficult as the bed was not very attractive to look at, but it was comfortable, and we could raise her head slightly, so it helped her sleep.

We continued to use the long, memory foam "wedge positioning pillow" that allowed Sue to lean against as she slept on her side.

Sue continued to sleep upstairs until mid-2017 when it became too difficult for her to use the stairlift.

Dawn raid by the police

October 2016 to December 2016

Relaxing in the Horseshoe Pub in Longlane
near Ashbourne celebrating Christmas
December 2016

Dawn raid by the police

October 2016 to December 2016

Looking back I realise that the signs were there in early August. It started with a breakdown in trust with one of the carers. The carer decided she could not continue and left.

There were some strange remarks made by Sue. After 21 years of marriage she became suspicious of me staying away on business. There were comments about me being a terrible carer and me wanting to put her into a care home. I really struggled with this. I was doing my best and trust is one of my core values, yet she was questioning this. The breakdown of Sue's trust then began to spread.

She started to make other accusations. Minor at first, then becoming worse. She said the carers and I were getting her medication wrong, that her food and drinks did not taste right, and that people were being rough.

I needed to go on a training course for work in Oxford and organised some night cover. I phoned home on the Monday night, but I knew something was wrong by the way the carers spoke. I said I would come home but they assured me all was well.

On the Tuesday morning it was clear it had been a difficult night, but again I was reassured that nothing was wrong. Later that night I received a panicked call from the carers. Sue was outside the house and was refusing to go back in. She was accusing the carers of trying to poison her. I tried to reassure her over the phone that it was all right, but she did not believe me. I called our neighbour and he told Sue that he would look after her and make sure she was safe. Trusting him she went back in the house and he stayed with her until she fell asleep. In the meantime, I left the course and rushed home.

The rest of the week was less eventful although Sue continued to make subtle comments. She called our friends repeating the accusations and we were all concerned. After speaking to the GP, we agreed to monitor the situation.

The following week I had to be at a leadership conference near our home, so I was still able to check on Sue. On doing so a carer told me that she had phoned someone called Hargreaves Lansdown. I was immediately concerned as this was not a person but our stockbroker.

Upon contacting them they confirmed my worst fears. She had told them to sell all our shares. When I asked Sue why she had done this she said that "people" were after her money. Fortunately, I was able to stop most of the sales.

Over the next two days Sue started to get more paranoid.

She repeatedly accused me of giving her the wrong medication, poisoning her food and drink, and trying to hurt her. I found this very difficult to hear and I was struggling to stay focussed at work. The GP was planning to visit on Thursday to see us, but this was starting to feel like a long way away.

Her perception of reality was now completely different to mine. She would watch me pour a glass of water, insisting somehow that I had poisoned it. I would drink from the cup and she told me that I had switched it even though it was in her sight the whole time. I could not comprehend this at all, it was so surreal.

On Wednesday night I was woken by banging on the front door. It was 3am. Half asleep I wandered downstairs. Through the front door I could see the police.

Fearing the worst, I opened the door. A policeman led me into the lounge and asked politely but assertively, what had been happening. In the meantime, the policewomen went upstairs. I did not know what he was talking about.

At around 2.30am Sue had called the police. Shouting down the phone she said that I was trying to hurt and poison her, that I was dealing drugs and flying them in and out of the country on the company private jet. They had tried to phone back, but no one answered. As Sue had not been sleeping, I had put the phone on silent so that she would not be disturbed.

Fearing the worst, the police had raced to the house with blue lights flashing and sirens wailing.

When the policewoman had gone upstairs, she had found Sue asleep. Upon waking Sue didn't believe that she was a real policewoman and accused her of being "in on it" with me.

I explained what had been happening over the last two weeks and we discussed the help they could provide and some suggestions for the next steps.

Although the whole experience had been scary and confusing the police could not have been more supportive and caring.

Later that morning the GP agreed that an assessment was needed. In the afternoon our GP, an approved Mental Health Practitioner, and a Community Psychiatrist visited us. They decided that Sue needed to be hospitalised and assessed under Section 2 of the Mental Health Act. I felt really guilty, as if I was letting Sue down in some way, but it was clear she needed help which I could not give her.

Refusing to go to the hospital with me, an ambulance was called. I was worried that this would be traumatic however the ambulance crew reassured Sue, telling her that they wanted to take her to safety. She was so happy that someone believed her that she went willingly.

She was then taken to accident and emergency rather than directly to a mental health unit. On the way I phoned our consultant and explained what was happening. He advised that I must ensure that she was admitted to an older adult, rather than adult, unit as they would be better equipped to handle her physical symptoms and it would be a calmer environment for her.

The strange thing about Sue's mental health was that it fluctuated. As anticipated the medics wanted to transfer her to the adult unit but I insisted it should be the older adult one. Interestingly when Sue arrived in A&E, she seemed normal resulting in them wanting to discharge her, as she was "clearly" better. An impasse ensued and I refused. In the end she was admitted into a general hospital ward whilst we agreed the right course of action.

This was when the fun started.

A couple of days later I was sitting with the psychiatrist liaison officer when her pager went off, but the message was for me, not her, to return to the ward. We found Sue in her wheelchair in the middle of the ward entrance. She had persuaded a nurse to take her for a ride and then stuck her hands in the spokes refusing to move any further. At that moment two porters were trying to move a bed with a new patient onto the ward and Sue had blocked their way. To make the situation even more dramatic she had chosen to do this just as visiting hours started. As a result, there were visitors standing waiting to get past. Every time someone went close to her, she would scream. She was effectively staging a sit-in.

Within 24 hours she was transferred to the older adult mental health unit.

Arriving at the mental health unit we were greeted by the resident psychiatrist. Unlike other hospital admissions Sue was being sectioned and detained so he had to explain her rights.

The psychiatrist gave Sue a leaflet on what was happening and her sectioning papers. Sue was not impressed. As he tried to read them, she tore them up and threw them back at him. Apparently, this was the first time someone had done that to him.

"I think that tells you what she thinks about that then," I said and laughed. I know I should not have laughed but it was the stress of the last few weeks that triggered it.

He suggested Sue had something to eat. One of the staff bought some minced beef and potatoes. Sue took one look at it, "It looks like s*!t." (And I must admit it did).

I said, "I am sure it tastes better than it looks".

She took a mouthful and spat it out "It tastes like– ".

Managing to interrupt her I asked if they had something different. Fish and chips were bought which had clearly been under the warming lamp for too long and were dry.

Sue opened her mouth to say something and I again interrupted and asked if they had anything else. Sponge and custard was then put in front of Sue, which had also been under the warming lamp for too long.

I decided to pre-empt her. "If you do not eat this then I will."

My words obviously triggered some deep-rooted feeling that it was better she ate it rather than me and Sue started to eat it. Every spoonful drew a face similar to a baby trying solids for the first time.

Having "safely navigated" the first 30 minutes of our time in the mental health unit the Psychiatrist said it was time for me to go. Their preference was to let Sue settle in over the next five days and then I could visit.

The following morning, I got a call asking if I could come in to help. Sue was being difficult and refusing to eat any food or take her medication. Over the next two weeks I visited morning and evening, bringing food.

At the end of the two weeks I was informed that Sue was much better. I was sceptical but they assured me she was well enough to return home. As we discussed the situation it became clear to me that Sue was using her knowledge from her Psychology degree to give all the answers they were looking for. Further treatment was needed.

Sue was in the unit for four weeks until mid-December. The cause of her psychosis was the interaction and strength of the drugs with a little bit related to her illness progressing. As the doctors took her off the drugs, restarted them and tried different combinations it became clear that she was struggling to tolerate the one of the Parkinson's medications (a dopamine-receptor agonist that mimics the action of dopamine which is responsible for smooth, purposeful movement and is deficient in people with MSA and Parkinson's disease).

≈

Whilst Sue was in the mental health unit, for the first time she went into a very deep, unresponsive sleep.

When I approached her bedside, she did not stir. As I watched her sleep I was concerned and tried to wake her up. A doctor tried pinching her ear lobe and other techniques, but she would not wake up. Her ECG, blood pressure and blood tests were normal.

An ambulance was called to transfer her to A&E.

As we discussed what was happening Sue suddenly woke up and started speaking, making all of us jump. She was totally unaware of what had happened and how she had arrived in A&E. We never got to the bottom of what was causing this, but it happened subsequently on several occasions.

≈

Psychosis is a rare symptom for MSA but is more common in other illnesses that have similar symptoms to MSA. Our lead consultant and I had a conversation about whether the diagnosis of MSA-P was correct and if there was an alternative diagnosis. Other illnesses that are similar to MSA-P include:

- MSA-C which has more cerebellar (coordination) related symptoms, some of which Sue had, but her parkinsonian symptoms were more prevalent.

- Dementia with Lewy Bodies (DLB) has the same movement and autonomic issues as MSA but typically visual hallucinations at an early stage. We were not sure if Sue was seeing things as part of her psychosis. In DLB there is also usually cognitive decline, but Sue's memory seemed razor sharp.

- Progressive supranuclear palsy (PSP) has the same symptoms as MSA but typically involves loss of concentration or poor attention span and a struggle with visual information. Sue did not have these before the psychosis, but she certainly struggled at times to watch longer TV programmes as her MSA progressed.

- Corticobasal syndrome (CBS) has movement issues but typically involves language problems, which Sue did not have.

We concluded that MSA-P was still the most likely diagnosis, but it was worth considering alternative options. This was important to us as we needed to be able to put a label on Sue's illness and it might have affected the anticipated symptoms, treatment or outcome.

≈

I was relieved when Sue was finally discharged. She was back to her normal self.

I had found the whole experience frightening. It was the time I struggled the most. I did not understand why she no longer trusted me. Despite everything I was doing she did not appreciate me. As she made accusations, I worried that someone would believe them. I was worried about the carers or me losing our jobs or even worse. I was even more worried about Sue and what was going to happen. I could tell she was scared too but nothing I said or did calmed her down.

I now appreciate what it is like to live with someone who has mental health issues. It was much harder than the physical care, which was challenging enough.

Sue was now feeling better. Strangely she could not remember any of the events leading up to her admission, nor the first few weeks of her stay in the mental health unit.

On discharge we were assigned a community psychiatric nurse. She met Sue on a regular basis throughout the rest of our journey, keeping an eye on her mental state. She also kept an eye on me.

We slowly reduced the anti-depression and anti-psychosis drugs to a minimum level. These really helped Sue but other people's attitude to these drugs was interesting.

I lost count of the number of people who warned me about the drugs, their side-effects and their addictiveness without knowing anything about them. It was then that I really became aware of the stigma attached to mental health episodes and the use of drugs. The reality is that these are extremely effective and, if used properly, without significant risk of addiction.

My simple advice is that if you are experiencing mental or emotional issues then reach out for help just as you would do if you had a physical issue.

≈

Jan was keen to keep doing things with Sue after the mental health issue so, as Christmas approached, she invited Sue to "Sherry in the Shed" to celebrate. Jan's daughters had decorated the shed with fairy lights, put two chairs in with rugs to keep warm and made a homemade soup. Holding Sue's hands to keep her steady, I walked her to the bottom of the garden. Two hours, a flask of soup and half a bottle of sherry later she walked back in a perfectly straight line – the alcohol-induced stagger counteracting perfectly the unsteadiness caused by MSA.

One of the issues we identified during the mental health episode was that being married does not give each of you an automatic right to deal with each other's affairs. For example, the bank would not provide me access to information on Sue's savings accounts even though I just wanted to check she had not done anything strange. I was repeatedly told that I needed a lasting power of attorney (LPA).

Sue arranged for a solicitor to talk to her about granting me an LPA. There are two types of LPA: health and welfare, and property and financial affairs. These are legal documents that allowed me to act on her behalf. The health and welfare LPA would only come into effect when she was unable to make decisions or not able to act on her decisions because of, for example, issues with communication. The financial LPA could be used on registration, with Sue's permission.

Sue continued to be involved in all the decisions throughout our journey but having the LPAs in place allowed me to act on her behalf as she increasingly lost the ability to interact with people naturally due to mobility and communication challenges.

Organising the LPAs early is important. It allows the person with MSA to be in control when the LPAs are discussed, agreed and signed. As the whole process can take eight to ten weeks, doing it early also means they are in place ahead of them being needed.

At the same time as putting the LPAs in place we contacted the GP practice and registered myself as a primary carer so I could discuss all her medical needs as her communication became more difficult and stressful. It also provided access to support, e.g. prioritised GP appointments.

The power of makeup

January 2017 to June 2017

Sue having a sneaky shot with Gemma on one of the last nights that she was able to eat and drink out.
February 2017

The power of makeup

January 2017 to June 2017

The first half of 2017 saw another decline in Sue's condition after a period of relative stability. In January she still had a small amount of strength in her legs and would occasionally use a walker, but she was increasingly dependent on the wheelchair.

From early February she needed my help if she wanted to have a bath, shower or wash her hair. We bought an inflatable seat for the bath so she could be lowered into the bath and raised back out. We also bought a shower chair.

By March Sue started losing the dexterity in her hands. She struggled to put her contact lenses in and could not apply make-up or cut her nails.

In April transfers between the bed, stairlift, wheelchair, and the car, were becoming increasingly harder and riskier for myself, the carers and Sue. I had to make sure she was downstairs before I left for work as the carers were unable to help her onto the stairlift.

She started to struggle to swallow, became much slower eating and drinking, and as a result, was consuming less and started to lose weight. Her incontinence also had become worse and she had to start wearing incontinence pants rather than pads.

In April the dieticians recommended that a small feeding tube called a gastrostomy was fitted. The tube would connect directly into Sue's stomach cavity and enable food, fluids and medicine to be consumed directly so she did not have to struggle to swallow or worry about choking. A gastrostomy can be installed by one of two ways, using an endoscope or x-ray. The former is known as a PEG, the latter is known as a RIG (radiologically inserted gastrostomy). As Sue was struggling to lie down and her head was leaning forwards the only option was x-ray guided.

Sue was reluctant to have this done and was worried about how it would look. She was especially worried that it might trigger her Crohn's Disease to return. So, we held back.

By June she was really struggling with food. There was no option but to have the RIG fitted. The procedure was very simple and straight forward and you could not see the tube under her clothes.

I was given 10 minutes of training on how to feed Sue through the tube and how to unblock it if there were any problems. It felt daunting at the time, but I soon became an "expert" in how to use a RIG, keep it clean, and unblock it if there was a problem.

Sue was prescribed Nutrison Soya Feed, which contains all the necessary nutrients and vitamins. It is a liquid that goes through the RIG tube directly into the stomach and takes the stress out of eating through the mouth and any fears around swallowing. Sue gained and maintained her weight, and her blood test results were always perfect. The RIG was also used for her medication and fluids.

There was one disadvantage of the RIG. To perform a feed could take anywhere between 10 and 20 minutes. During that time, we had to hold a funnel (actually a 60ml syringe with the plunger removed) at chest height. Gravity would then push the liquid through the tube. We constantly refilled the syringe until 300ml of liquid food had gone through the tube. This had to be repeated six to seven times a day. The medication was done separately, 30 minutes before or after the feed. The result was that the carers or I had to hold the syringe up to ten times per day. All of us developed muscles that we did not know existed! More importantly I learnt patience, as this process could not be rushed.

There were three further challenges with using the RIG:

1. The NHS only gives out a small number of syringes per month and they need to be sterilised after each use. I noticed that Sue had an increase in urinary infections after we started RIG feeding. I do not know whether this was related or not, but we switched to "use once" syringes and that seemed to improve the situation.

2. We were putting all of Sue's medication through the tube. This involved crushing tablets, opening capsules, and liquid medication. If we did not crush the tablets, then the tube could block, and it was sometimes impossible to unblock without needing to visit A&E.

3. We had to make sure that the tube did not get pulled out by accident. The feeding tube has a balloon that sits inside the stomach and should prevent this, but it came out three times as the balloon kept deflating.

By June it became too difficult to get Sue in and out of bed on my own. Each time I helped her I was risking her and my health. The only option was to start using a standing aid. This is a device that provides assistance for people who still have enough strength in their legs to stand but not enough to stand up or sit down. The problem is that the standing aid needs enough room around the bed and is on wheels so does not work very well on thick carpet.

We decided it was time for Sue to start sleeping downstairs. This was a difficult decision and another milestone on the journey. To help reduce the feeling of isolation we moved a bed into the dining room so I could sleep downstairs when Sue wanted company.

Sue had also stopped using the walker and was totally dependent on the wheelchair. This was not a conscious decision but rather something that just happened over time. Whilst this conserved her energy and was safer for her we were now struggling to get her in and out of our car.

≈

Maintaining intimacy as a couple is challenging with any illness let alone MSA. It affects how you connect emotionally, physically and intellectually. It affects your interests, your roles in each other's lives, your trust in one another, and it tests your commitment. It also affects you spiritually as you all consider the progression of the illness and the eventual outcome.

Despite the challenges of those changes (or perhaps because of them) I believe that we became closer as a couple.

I put a lot of effort and focus on maintaining the intimacy of our relationship and trying to avoid the trap of becoming a "carer" or "distant". This was difficult at times, especially as Sue's communication capabilities diminished.

≈

As a couple we were finely tuned into each other's emotions. Sue often seemed to sense how I was feeling even before I knew myself. We were so similar yet also very different in many ways.

To continue the emotional intimacy, I would frequently buy her flowers, light scented candles, listen to music with her, and constantly told her that I loved her which I did and always will.

She remained upbeat and positive throughout the illness but as it progressed, I could occasionally see subtle changes in her emotions. We would talk about these and I would try and reassure her.

Sometimes her emotions would not reflect how she was really feeling. A little known and talked about symptom of MSA is that it can create emotional lability in a small minority of people with MSA. This is where there is a rapid and exaggerated change in mood that is not reflective of how they are feeling or the situation, e.g. laughing at something that is sad. Constantly checking that Sue was okay ensured I could spot these rare moments and help her express her emotions more accurately.

The exceptional carers showed great empathy and could also tune into Sue's emotions. In these situations, I would find post-it notes stuck on the wall when I arrived home letting me know the issue (and what I had forgotten to do, for example, organising a trip out or buying something).

For a small number of people, another emotional impact from MSA and the drugs used are changes in compulsive and impulsive behaviours.

Our consultant had warned us to watch out for gambling addictions when he had confirmed MSA back in early 2015. As we walked out of the room Sue had turned to me.

"I bet that won't happen." She said.

I burst out laughing "It already had."

Another dimension to this was hypersexuality. This manifested itself by Sue becoming flirtatious. If a good-looking young man happened to come into range, she suddenly had a twinkle in her eye and a seductive smile. It became a game with the carers, which I must admit to encouraging as it made her happy.

I became more aware of my own emotional state as Sue could easily pick up how I was feeling, and I did not want to cause her more anxiety. I found the MSA journey a roller coaster of a ride. At times I was able to cope with everything that was thrown at me but at other times I really struggled.

The biggest emotional challenge for me at the start was managing to remain patient. I had to learn to slow down so that Sue did not feel pressured when getting dressed or when doing tasks such as the RIG feed.

Another challenge was overcoming my guilt.

I felt guilty that I was healthy and that I was still able to do and enjoy normal things as Sue struggled with a progressive illness.

I felt guilt whenever I got frustrated with the situation.

And I felt most guilty that I could not get the right balance between all the things going on in my life. Perhaps I could have done better as a carer if I had just focussed providing care. At the same time, perhaps I could have done better at work or been a better friend to others. I know that I de-prioritised my own health and welfare to look after Sue.

Eventually I realised that there is simply not enough time in the day or enough energy to do everything. Ultimately life is a balancing act, about making difficult choices and compromises. You just have to try and get the balance right but even now I look back and wonder "what if…"

It is very easy to get frustrated when living with someone who has a serious illness. It changes everything. It stopped me doing the things I normally did. Our house became filled with things that were a constant reminder of the battle. My thoughts became focussed on caring for Sue. I was reactive to what was happening. I got incredibly tired and had limited, if any, time to myself. It totally dominated me, and perhaps even started to redefine who I was.

I reminded myself constantly that this was not Sue's fault. I never got angry, annoyed or frustrated with her and I certainly never blamed her for anything that was happening. I did though get frustrated with the behaviour of others. My mantra of "treating people like you want to be treated yourself" is clearly is not shared by everyone. So, when I became frustrated, I talked it through with my family and friends.

≈

When people talk about physical intimacy some people, well my male friends, titter and think of the physical act of sex. It is fair to say that MSA does have an impact on being physically intimate, however there is so much more to intimacy than sex.

I was keen to ensure that Sue knew there was no change in how I felt about her. I wanted her to still feel the same about herself. We maintained a physical connection by holding hands, hugging, cuddling, kissing and me reinforcing my feelings with the simplest and gentlest of touches.

The illness presented new opportunities for us to build and maintain physical and emotional intimacy.

The main one for us was the Saturday morning routine. It started with me getting Sue undressed, using a hoist, I would then move her from the bed and onto an Arjohuntleigh Carendo multi-purpose hygiene chair. The chair could then be used to reposition Sue from sitting to lying down. I then raised her up to the right height for me to do a shower and hair wash without having to bend over. The race was then on to dry and dress her before she got cold.

It was then that I discovered three hidden talents:

1. Hairdressing. I can blow dry a lady's hair, use curling tongues to straighten or create curls, do ponytails and even braid.

2. Makeup. I have no idea how I learnt to do this but I know how to use cleansers and moisturisers; apply foundation; use concealer; add colour through blusher and bronzer; emphasise eyes with different shades of eye shadow, eye liner and mascara; apply finishing touches with lip stick.

   (I even have favourite products. I loved the NARS Goa eye shadow. The green really made Sue's blue eyes stand out.)

3. Manicures. I used a nail varnish with a magnet in the lid (this produced amazing results as the nail varnish had miniscule pieces of metal that then follow the shape of the magnet to create patterns as the nail varnish dried). I also bought a nail painting kit (with slightly more haphazard results).

The whole process could take a few hours, but the Saturday morning routine was the only time that Sue and I were truly on our own. It became a special and precious time. It created a strong physical connection as it was so personal. I enjoyed it as much as Sue. It helped her maintain the high standards she had before the illness and made her feel attractive. The reality is she did not need this in my eyes. She was always, and remained, beautiful throughout the illness.

The carers often said that if my career in IT did not work out then I could forge one as a make-up artist to the stars.

≈

It is very easy to make all the decisions especially as someone starts to struggle to communicate, however MSA does not normally affect mental capacity or memory. I made sure that Sue remained an equal intellectual partner and continued to make key decisions, especially about her care and how we spent our time together. To help her do this we made sure we created the time to allow her to communicate her thoughts and ideas, always checking to make sure we had fully understood her wishes.

≈

One of the key elements of intimacy in a relationship is sharing common interests and experiences.

Sue's favourite "hobby" was clothes shopping and I was an ideal partner having been trained as a child by my mum as she "dragged" my sister and me around the shops while dad worked or played golf.

Sue also loved our garden and making it as nice as possible. She would spend hours designing the garden and choosing plants. I would then spend even more time doing the landscaping and planting. We enjoyed watching television, going on walks, and cooking together. Our favourite chef was Yotam Ottolenghi and we regularly tried recipes out of his cookbooks.

I was determined that we would continue to do things together. This was a key factor in us coping with the challenges of MSA. Amongst all the things we did in the first half of 2017 there were four highlights:

- The first was in the last week of February when we went out with friends for a meal. This would be the last time that Sue would be able to eat and drink in a restaurant. The picture at the start of this chapter is Sue having a sneaky shot during the evening and is one of my favourite pictures during the MSA journey.

- The second highlight was two weeks later. We went to Katie and Warren's wedding. They are a wonderful couple and made Sue feel so welcome. Katie is one of the many friends who rallied around me when Sue passed away.

- The third highlight was the annual Duffield Carnival. With Sue in the wheelchair we went to support our friend Jan as she had entered the Women's Institute Victoria Sponge competition. Jan won 3rd prize (in my humble opinion she should have won).

- The final highlight was experienced in a different way for Sue. At the time I was running the IT department for Rolls-Royce. We had entered the UK Women in IT awards and been shortlisted. The

> awards night was a black-tie event in London, and I was accompanied by some of the great female IT leaders in my team. Sue would have gone with us, but unfortunately it was just too difficult to organise. Wanting her to be part of the awards night, I was constantly video calling her and sent photos throughout the night.
>
> The host was Maggie Philbin. Sitting on the edge of the seats we were delighted when she announced Rolls-Royce had won the Women in IT "employer of the year" category. It recognised all the hard work we had done around diversity and inclusion. I have been blessed to have three strong, inspirational and influential women in my life: Sue, my mum and my sister. They actively encouraged me to take a lead on this important topic and were all so proud when we won.

I constantly used video calls and took videos and photos when I was away on trips, so Sue felt more part of my life. As the illness progressed the ability to do this meant that her experiences were not limited to what was happening in the house or to the short trips we were doing together.

≈

I will not dwell too much on trust and commitment other than to say that I had promised Sue that I would look after her and ensure she was able to stay at home for the entire MSA journey.

To me it was something that I never doubted. I never broke a promise I made to her, but a major illness makes you feel more vulnerable, so I constantly reassured her of my commitment and met it fully.

≈

Sue and I had a strong spiritual connection, but I don't mean this in the religious sense. I felt this connection the first time I met her, but I did not understand it at the time. I just knew that I wanted to be with her.

Our conversations would flow freely but we were equally comfortable just being together in silence. We had an ability to communicate what we were thinking or feeling without speaking.

We had an incredible bond, our lives were enriched and enhanced by each other and we always put the other one first. I felt I could be myself but equally felt myself growing in a positive way through Sue's influence.

We supported each other in every aspect of our lives. Irrespective of what was happening there was a calmness that we brought to each other. We shared the same values and moral compass.

It was this spiritual connection that made Sue's illness so hard and at the same time so easy to cope with.

A close call

July 2017 to December 2017

Sue focussed on using the Eye Gaze screen and software before asking the NHS Clinical Scientist to make yet another visit to calibrate the device.

October 2017

A close call

July 2017 to December 2017

Sue developed a chest infection at the start of July. The GP prescribed some antibiotics that did not work.

She was taken into hospital and throughout the next week different antibiotics were tried. Her health deteriorated with rapidly rising temperature, high respiratory rate, abnormally high heartbeat, low oxygen levels and poor blood test results. Severe sepsis was diagnosed but they were running out of options.

I was warned that it was touch and go; I should be prepared for the worst. A last throw of the dice worked as the final antibiotic took hold and the infection subsided. I had not left her bedside for those two weeks and was exhausted physically and mentally.

As there was concern about future chest infections, Sue was referred to the community respiratory physiotherapists. They identified that she was not taking deep breaths and the volume of air entering her lungs was therefore low.

The physiotherapists recommended the use of a Lung Volume Recruitment (LVR) bag. This is a flexible plastic bag with a mask that Sue used to perform breathing exercises to take in more air.

As a result, there was never a repeat of the chest infection that was such a close call.

≈

It was now too difficult to transfer Sue safely from the wheelchair into the car, so we decided to lease a used Wheelchair Accessible Vehicle (WAV) using the mobility part of PIP.

The Jubilee Automotive Group in Birmingham has an extensive range of vehicles and we were able to try out different ones. This was important as Sue was using the Invacare Rea Azalea. This chair tilts and reclines and is quite a large wheelchair to fit in a vehicle.

We wanted a vehicle with an "up front wheelchair" configuration, which means the space for the wheelchair is in the front alongside the driver. This enabled Sue to sit next to me so that we still felt connected and she was able to look out of the windscreen. There was a single seat behind the driver so a carer could join us when we needed support.

We also needed a vehicle that had easy access for the wheelchair. We selected a used Volkswagen Caddy that had an electric ramp and rear suspension that lowered to help get Sue into the vehicle. However, it still required a lot of manual effort to push Sue up the ramp. I also had to secure the wheelchair manually using some straps. Both these tasks can be done electronically in some vehicles, which is worth considering to reduce the manual effort.

The carers called the WAV our "Party Bus" as it allowed us to continue going out on day trips, visit friends' houses, and go out to parties and nightclubs. To complete the picture,

I bought disco lights that plugged into the cigarette lighter and often played loud music when we went out.

The WAV also made attending hospital appointments so much easier. With hindsight getting the WAV was one of the best decisions we made.

≈

Sue's wrists had involuntary flexion (bending inwards) and her dexterity was now getting worse. Her feet were also showing signs of plantar flexion (foot drop). Both are forms of dystonia, an involuntary contracting of the muscles. It was a bit like getting cramp all the time but thankfully Sue did not suffer any pain from this.

To take the pressure off her joints we introduced splints for hand, wrist and lower arm. These were created specifically for her posture and we continued to use cushions or rolled up towels to support her feet.

As the dystonia symptoms progressed, we frequently reshaped the splints and she started having Botox injections. Twice weekly massages also really helped as these not only relaxed the muscles but were also enjoyable.

Sue found that her hands and feet were frequently cold, and she started wearing fingerless gloves all the time. We also put an extra cover on her feet. However, with MSA, there are fluctuations in body temperature, so we had to constantly check whether she was too hot or cold as she was unable to take the covers off herself.

≈

September came with another awards night. I was nominated for CIO of the Year and I went to London. Again, Sue couldn't go with me, so I used a video call once more to involve her in the event.

She was so excited when we won. I say "we" deliberately as I could not have achieved what I have done in my career without Sue by my side, giving me the wisdom of her advice and guidance throughout.

≈

Sue and I were blessed with amazing experiences that were offered as part of doing my job. We stayed in Windsor Castle for a week as part of a training programme and we were entertained at the William Paca House, owned by one of the four signatories on the Declaration of Independence, which included a private tour of the National Aquarium in Baltimore.

In October I was offered an opportunity to attend an event at the Palais de Versailles in Paris to celebrate the 50th Anniversary of a supplier. I declined because Sue could not go. She was mortified, insisted I should accept and eventually I agreed.

On the 5th of October, wearing a tuxedo, I found myself on the red carpet arriving at the Palais de Versailles. Walking down the red carpet I was greeted by trumpeters dressed in uniforms from the 1700s. As I continued through the Palace and out into the gardens there were musicians playing Baroque music.

As the sun set, with a glass of champagne in my hand, a fantastic firework display started the evening's entertainment.

We moved into the Orangery, a very long room, with over 100 tables. I was on table 99 so expected to be seated at the back. As I walked to the table, I found I was actually on one of the two main tables.

I had an amazing meal, and unbeknownst to me, spent part of the evening talking to Tony Hadley of Spandau Ballet. He then entertained the guests by singing several of his hits. It was a great finish to the evening and Sue had been able to enjoy it too as I had relayed most of the evening to her via my phone.

In mid-October, and continuing the theme of fireworks, we visited Matlock Bath, a small town in Derbyshire. It is nestled in a beautiful gorge along the river Derwent. A popular destination for families and motorcyclists, the highlight for us was the Matlock Bath Illuminations. Every year they decorate the riverside and light up the cliffs with a stunning display.

For the last 120 years, the Matlock Bath Venetian Boat Builders Association have built a wide variety of themed boats, brightly lit with an array of colours. These are then rowed down the river at night, creating a magical and enchanting scene.

My favourite was a paddle steamer, but Sue preferred the pirate ship. When the winner of the competition was announced it was Sue's choice that won, and when we revisited in 2018, she, once again, identified the winner as the best boat before the judges made their decision. She should have been on the judging panel! The evening finished with a spectacular firework display.

Inspired by the fireworks at the Palais de Versailles and Matlock Bath we hosted a firework display at our house on the 5th of November.

Having advertised the event as rivalling Paris and Matlock Bath, our family, friends and neighbours arrived with eager anticipation.

I'm not sure that our "5 metre distance" fireworks met their expectations, but I will never forget the moment I held Sue's hand as we made shapes and spelt her name with the sparklers.

We rounded off the evening with a homemade chilli-con-carne and jacket potatoes. It was a perfect night.

≈

By December Sue's speech had gone to a whisper. We could just about make out what she was saying. Most healthcare professionals described it as barely audible and visitors struggled to understand. Sue became increasingly tired as she made the effort to try to communicate.

The speech and language therapists (SALT) introduced a variety of techniques and tools to help. It started by removing superfluous words from sentences to reduce the effort in speaking.

As it became more difficult to make out the words Sue spoke the therapists introduced alphabet and communication charts that have individual letters and phrases printed on paper. They were simple to use as Sue would point at a phrase or spell out a sentence, but they made conversations very slow and some people had a real challenge turning the letters into words and sentences. Creating the time to have the conversation, showing patience and writing down the letters as they were pointed at really helped.

The SALT team trialled the use of eye tracking software. At this point a young male NHS clinical scientist entered our lives. He suggested an LC Technology Eyegaze Edge device which tracks eye movement and allows the user to spell out words and select phrases that are then spoken by the computer. The user can browse the internet and write emails as well.

The device requires careful calibration, so he had to return many times to set it up and show Sue how to use it. On his 20th visit he said to me, "Sue always gives me a massive smile when I walk in, but she must be very disappointed with me as I'm really struggling to get this set up to her satisfaction."

I didn't have the heart to tell him that it was more likely that she kept calling him back because he was very good looking. Thankfully the Eyegaze software could not interpret the message in her eyes when he walked into the room as that would have made him, and everyone else, feel a bit awkward.

The reality was that Sue struggled to use the eye tracking technology because of her head position, the accuracy of her eye movement, and the need to wear sunglasses to reduce glare and help with vision. As a result, the alphabet and communication charts became her main method of communication.

≈

We also had our first appointment with the Palliative Care services in December.

Being referred to this team was both worrying and scary. I knew that Sue had a progressive and terminal illness, and that we had just had a close call with the chest infection, but it felt as though someone was saying she did not have long to live.

I could not have been more wrong.

The palliative care consultant and team were very reassuring. They get involved in all types of illness, not just terminal ones, and they help at any stage of an illness. Their focus was on improving quality of life and they provided great advice in a supportive way.

They helped us to discuss some of the issues we needed to think about such as the ReSPECT (Recommended Summary Plan for Emergency Care and Treatment) form. This describes the treatment to be performed in the event of an emergency. They arranged for an emergency medicine pack to be in the house containing pain relief should Sue need it.

≈

December also saw an "unwelcome" addition. One of the carers bought Sue a wall calendar filled with half-dressed firemen and it had pride of place, so she saw it every time she woke up. I was not sure about this development but for some strange reason Sue and the carers looked forward to the first of each month in 2018, 2019 and 2020 (and yes someone bought one every year)!

Three colours

January 2018 to June 2018

Sue and I just before we lifted her into the new car
she had bought for my 50th Birthday.

Three colours

January 2018 to June 2018

Around ten years previously Sue had wanted to move closer to her parents. I was happy to go along with the plan, especially as part of the agreement was that we would take a larger mortgage in order to purchase my dream car: a Porsche. One day. returning home from work, I discovered that Sue had sold our house and made an offer on a new property. She had, unfortunately, agreed a price over our agreed limit, which meant the Porsche was no longer viable.

Back to January 2018, and I was fast approaching 50 years old. I decided it was now or never to buy a Porsche. Sue knew it was a childhood dream and that if I didn't do it now then it might never happen. Sue decided she wanted to buy one for me.

I was so excited when we arrived at the showroom. I explained to the salesman that I wanted Sue to be a key part of the selection process but that she was not able to talk. It was at that point I became surplus to the decision-making process other than to move Sue around in the wheelchair. Sue rejected car after car with a big thumbs down until she saw a Panamera Estate. A smile grew across her face and I felt as if I had won the lottery.

As we went through the car specification Sue used a thumb up or thumb down to signal what she wanted. I did have to tilt her thumb down when we were told the price of the black alloy wheels. After nearly an hour the car was ordered. The salesman showed an admirable amount of patience and empathy (though his commission may have been something to do with it).

My only concern was that Sue had chosen a bright blue car with red seats and green brake callipers. As we waited for the car to be delivered and I thought about it arriving, the blue became bluer, the red redder, and the green greener. I now feared that it was going to look like I was having a full-blown midlife crisis.

When we finally took ownership of my car, I should never have doubted Sue's eye for colour. Surprising both the salesman and I, it looked amazing.

I was determined that Sue would share in the excitement of picking up the new car. We arrived at the dealership in the Party Bus along with our standing aid. We then used it to transfer Sue from her wheelchair into the Porsche.

Sue had previously been a cautious driver and passenger, but her inhibitions had lowered as a result of the illness, and likewise her tolerance of risk had increased. Suddenly I had a speed demon sitting next to me and egging me on as we drove home. We got back safely with a big smile on both our faces. The carer arrived "a little bit later" in the Party Bus.

≈

The illness progressed at different rates throughout our journey and the first half of 2018 saw a slowdown in the progression after a lot of change in 2017.

The biggest change was a deterioration in Sue's vision. She had always worn contact lenses to address short sightedness. There were significant changes though in the dioptres score (the measure of the eye's optical strength), which resulted in monthly eye tests and even then, she struggled to focus. On a hunch the optician tried a shaded lens, and this improved her vision as it reduced the glare.

From mid-2018 Sue always wore sunglasses no matter how much light or dark there was. I thought she looked pretty cool when we went out, and I think that she liked the fact she could look at all the good-looking guys without me or them knowing.

≈

March saw a different challenge with Sue's favourite hair salon. Whilst they had wheelchair friendly access, they were now struggling to wash Sue's hair because of the position of the sinks and Sue's inability to tilt her head.

One of the carers recommended an experienced hairdresser who was able to visit Sue at home. There were a couple of devices that she used which meant Sue did not need to recline her head and could have her hair washed in bed or reclined in the wheelchair. One was an inflatable shampoo basin and the other was a hair-washing tray.

The hairdresser visited every three months, ensuring that Sue continued to have a professional haircut and blow dry.

The success of the home hairdresser also led me to arrange a professional beauty therapist to visit Sue for facials and manicures. I made sure to factor these home visits into the budget as they clearly contributed to Sue's wellbeing as it was important to her that she kept up her appearance.

≈

From mid-April we started to have daily visits from the district nurse to administer the midday medication following a change to her medication regime. This also allowed us to quickly discuss any issues we were concerned about, for example, skin condition, urinary or PEG site infections, and changes to symptoms that required changes to her care.

≈

In May 2018 I celebrated my 50th Birthday.

With the help of family, friends and carers Sue had arranged an action-packed week, which made it a bittersweet celebration of a major milestone.

We had a BBQ with the party revolving around Sue in her bed. She organised a quad biking experience for 20 of my friends which ended up with one of them having a broken sternum and wrist, so he missed the evening meal at the sushi bar where Sue, once again, was the centre of the party. We video called him but he was so high on laughing gas that he could not remember where he was let alone us calling.

≈

Sue's birthday was coming up and I wondered what to do. It was too hard to go away like we used to. Then one of the carers mentioned that there were hotels that specialise in providing holidays for people who need specialist equipment and/or care assistance. She recommended a hotel in Blackpool as it had all the right facilities and the staff had been trained as carers.

On the 15th of June we packed the Party Bus and set off for Blackpool with one of our carers for a five-day break.

Sue was a massive Strictly Come Dancing fan and her highlight was visiting the famous ballroom where it is filmed. We watched as the dancers performed the tango, waltz and foxtrot to perfection whilst I reminded Sue that I had two left feet.

We also visited Blackpool Tower and watched the circus. The acrobatic show was incredible and the clowns so funny. At the interval a make-up artist sat in the middle of the circus ring painting faces. I found myself queuing in a line of 3- and 4-year olds so I could have my face painted. Returning triumphantly, I was greeted by Sue and the carer shaking their heads from side to side in dismay.

"What's wrong?" I asked.

I got a few strange looks as I spent the rest of the afternoon walking around Blackpool, and around an hour later I realised the truth: my face was painted as a clown with a big red nose.

Sue was tired after going to the circus and wanted to stay in the hotel but needed me to find a chic bar for the following night. Not trusting me to select the right one she asked the carer to go with me whilst the hotel's carers looked after her.

After an hour of walking around we finally found a potential bar. We sat down and the waiter came over.

"What would you like to drink?" he asked.

I asked for a lager and the carer asked for a soft drink "As I'm working." she said. "Just to be clear" I added, "I don't need to pay ladies to have a drink with me".

The waiter's eyebrows raised.

The carer blushed and stuttered "No it's not like that! I work for his wife. I'm her personal assistant.". "True," I replied "but my wife is in the hotel and doesn't know we are here. We might come back tomorrow night, but she mustn't know we have been here tonight!"

He raised his eyebrows even further.

"I'll pay cash to avoid any evidence," I said.

As we left, I poked my head back through the door. "Remember – we haven't been here!"

In the morning I told Sue all about the exchange with the waiter. We returned to the bar that night with Sue in on the joke. The waiter's face was a picture as the three of us entered. "You look familiar," I said. "Have we met before?".

"Er..." he stuttered. "No, I don't think so".

Sue, already smiling, burst out laughing. I apologised to the waiter for having a bit of fun at his expense, but it made the evening as we joked with him throughout the night.

We also visited the Pleasure Beach amusement park early one morning. As there were no queues, I was able to go on several rollercoasters. I think Sue enjoyed looking at me as I became increasingly unwell being constantly tossed from side to side and turned upside down. The full English breakfast had not been a good idea.

One of the benefits of the hotel was that it was at the quieter end of Blackpool. It had a tram stop directly outside and we had many enjoyable tram-rides.

Just prior to going to Blackpool I had been talking to our pharmacist about the upcoming trip. She had never visited so I described the Tower and illuminations. I mentioned the iconic hats with the "kiss me quick" slogan. She had never heard of it, so it became a mission to find one. It was a lot harder than I was expecting. At last I secured the required hat and gave it to the pharmacist as a present. I doubt it was ever worn but it bought a smile to her face and was a "nice" surprise for someone who helped us with the piles of medication that Sue needed on a regular basis.

We also spent several hours just sitting on the promenade watching the sea and the sun set. These moments were my highlight and I hate the fact that I will not watch another sunset with Sue.

A different lady every night

July 2018 to December 2018

Sue having a laugh with Raja on a night out with our friends, who tried to catch eggs in their hats at the local Japanese restaurant. Sue loved sushi so it was a regular haunt.

July 2018

A different lady every night

July 2018 to December 2018

There is definitely a problem when you go to sleep and you are not sure which lady is going to be there when you wake-up. First there was Vicky, then she was followed by Gemma, Monique, Rebecca, Victoria, Jess, Brookie, Lynn, Amy, Beckie, Grace, Jesse, Katie, Ashleigh, Elizabeth, Liz, Gemma, Natalie, Megan, Lizzie, Beni, Debbie, Denise, Holly, Michelle, Michelle, Thabani, Natalie, Amanda, Jody, Aana and Hannah.

That's even before I try to remember the ladies who turned up at my door at 10pm every night, introduced themselves before spending the night in the house, and then disappeared before morning. (I am not sure what I did but this happened a few times).

Before we arranged to have carers round the clock, I was providing the care throughout the night. My "shift" as the only carer would start at 8pm when the daytime team finished. I would take over having just walked in from work with barely any time to change my clothes.

Sue would normally need my help straight away and I would be busy until she fell asleep. If I was lucky, I would be able to eat a microwave meal or order a takeaway. I never had time to cook anything healthy nor do any exercise so rapidly put on weight. I knew that my health was suffering in order to make Sue's journey as bearable as possible.

I went to bed after midnight before being woken in the night by Sue pressing the buzzer and needing me to sort out something that would take an hour or more.

I would be awake again at 6.30am ready to repeat the daily routine including handing over to the daytime team that started at 7am.

At weekends it was worse, as the daytime team visits and hours were reduced, and I went into full time carer mode.

I was exhausted, physically and mentally.

Eventually I decided to arrange night-time care. I had to pay for this and arrange an MDT meeting to review the need and obtain some financial support.

The introduction of the night care team allowed me, for the first time in a couple of years, to have uninterrupted sleep (although Sue often insisted that the carers come and get me. Often it was simply to reassure her that everything was all right but there were times when there was a real problem that needed my help, for example, when her RIG feeding tube came out).

Due to the level of care that Sue needed, a lot of people came and went through our home. I lost privacy, especially when the night team started. They stayed awake looking after Sue and the noises they made initially disturbed my sleep, but I eventually got used to it.

To make things more challenging for the carers, Sue wanted to sleep listening to relaxing music. I am amazed they never dozed off.

I will forever be in the debt to these amazing ladies and the rest of the care team. Michelle and Hannah hold a particularly special place for me as they were with Sue and I in hospital on the preceding Friday and Saturday nights before she passed away. Knowing what was about to happen made these the longest and hardest nights I have suffered. Thanks to their support they made it slightly more bearable for us both.

≈

July was a really hot month and Sue was struggling with her temperature, swinging between extremely hot and very cold. We bought "water activated cooling towels" that really helped. We would often soak them in water, wring them out, and then place them on Sue's neck, arms or legs. They provided Sue with an instant, refreshing chill but they didn't make her wet. We also used cooling fans to help circulate the air and create a gentle breeze.

It was then that Sue decided she wanted to buy a LazySpa blow-up Jacuzzi so she could enjoy floating, the warmth and the bubbles. The problem was how to get her in and out as she couldn't support her own weight. That weekend we arranged with Steve, our builder, to build a platform for the Jacuzzi that enabled the legs of the hoist to go underneath.

To celebrate its first use, we poured a glass of champagne and Sue had a sip even though she could not hold the glass or swallow. To add to the mood, we turned on some romantic music and the inbuilt flashing coloured lights.

It would have been a perfect moment if it had not been for the two carers standing outside the Jacuzzi watching us to make sure I did not end up drowning Sue. We used buoyancy aids so that Sue could enjoy floating in the warmth and bubbles. She loved the experience as it helped with all the muscle stiffness.

My favourite times were doing this late at night. I put fairy lights around the Jacuzzi; staring at the stars sitting in 40-degree water was just perfect.

The downside was that we had to get Sue out first and make sure we showered and dried her before I could then get myself sorted.

Despite many offers, strangely I could never get any of the carers to join us in the Jacuzzi.

≈

July brought another awards ceremony but this one was different. Sue's carers had been nominated for several awards in the "Derbyshire Carer of the Year" competition. We headed to Pride Park Stadium, home of Derby County Football Club, and cheered the team on as they won some of the awards.

After the ceremony I was sitting talking to one of the managers when I realised that Sue and the carers had disappeared. Searching for them I came across them giggling and pointing out of the window. Approaching them unnoticed I found them watching Frank Lampard put the first team through a coaching session on the pitch. Typical.

Even at an awards ceremony, Sue had managed to find twenty plus fit young men in shorts to stare at.

≈

Sue had a routine dentist appointment in September, and we encountered the same issue as we had with the hairdresser. She was not able to get into a position that the dentist could deal with. Worse still, the dentist identified that Sue was grinding her teeth and that there were early signs of decay.

We were referred to the NHS Community Dental Services who specialise in providing dental services for those with complex needs.

After an initial assessment they prescribed a non-foaming, high fluoride toothpaste that the carers and I could use with Sue without the risk of her choking. At the time we were using mouth swabs (small sponges on sticks) to moisten Sue's mouth. She enjoyed them being dipped in cranberry juice, but the dentist felt that this was too acidic. The dentist suggested swapping to mint tea instead of the cranberry juice to reduce the erosion of the tooth enamel. Unfortunately, a mouthguard for the teeth grinding was not suitable.

We visited the dentist every three months to prevent the need for major dental work and they used temporary fillings to protect Sue's teeth. As a strategy it worked well, and we managed to keep Sue pain free.

≈

At the end of September, I had a friend over for breakfast and I went all out. I gave a bagel topped with smoked salmon, scrambled egg, and roasted vine tomatoes.

"That's the best breakfast I've ever had," he said.

"You know there's no such thing as a free meal," I replied. "I need you to help me to bake an apple crumble."

I climbed into one of our trees to get the best apples, and I swear that Sue smiled as I nearly fell out. As my friend never cooks it was a total nightmare, but we managed to cobble together a half decent crumble much to Sue's amusement.

Sue then decided we needed to go shopping so we headed to John Lewis in Nottingham, her favourite shop. We'd had many lunches there when we dated, and it always brought back memories of those times.

Returning in the Party Bus laden with bags, I put on Poker Face by Lady Gaga and turned on the disco lights. As we pulled up to some red traffic lights for roadworks, I wound down the window. Bouncing up and down in the driver's seat to the beat of the music I managed to get the van to bounce to the rhythm.

It was at that moment that a young cyclist rode towards us.

Spotting me, the van bouncing up and down, with music blaring out of the open window and disco lights flashing, the cyclist looked me in the eye, winked, smiled and shouted, "HELLO DARLING!"

Before I could reply the cyclist was gone.

Sue, hidden from view as she was reclined in the wheelchair, and the carer, also hidden from view because of the blacked-out windows, burst out laughing.

Turning to them I said, "Don't knock it, I've clearly still got it."

Sue simply looked at me, raised an eyebrow and without saying anything put me in my place. In her eyes I clearly did not!

Arriving home 15 minutes later, Sue and the carer were still laughing. Another carer, ready to start her shift, was waiting for us.

"What's happened?" she asked.

"Let me summarise," I told her. "I had someone over for breakfast, did some baking, went clothes shopping, danced in the van, and pulled a cyclist. I've clearly still got it."

Her response was simply a shake of the head and a raised eyebrow, which just triggered more laughter from them all.

I still smile when I hear that song. I wish the cyclist could know that with just a smile and a wink, they had made another fantastic memory for us on our journey.

≈

In October, Sue's wrists and fingers became more rigid; it was as if she had constant cramps. She never complained about these, but I knew that it must be painful, so we continued with regular massages.

I lost track of the hours I spent massaging her hands and fingers only to see them revert to the rigidity within minutes of stopping.

I was frustrated I could not give her the relief for long and would have happily swapped places just to be able to take the pain away.

Jan, our neighbour, freely gave her time, visiting Sue most days. Sometimes she would just sit holding Sue's hand as she slept. Other days she would tell Sue stories about what was happening. Most of the time they laughed at everything that was going on and some of the things said even made me blush.

It was around this time that Jan purchased a toy rat from Ikea and presented it to Sue.

"I saw this and thought of you", she said.

A strange gift and comment to give to a friend, however it was because Sue was clenching her fingers tightly and the rat was just the perfect size for Sue to hold and clench, avoiding her nails digging into her hand. Sue never let go of that rat.

Jan was also Sue's confidant and always looked after her best interests. She would not hesitate to tell me something that Sue wanted me to know, what wasn't working or what I could do better. It's impossible to see everything, especially when you're so close to the action. You need someone who can point things out that you may not see. She always did it out of love for Sue.

I know that Jan misses her daily visits to spend time with Sue.

≈

In November we had a follow-up appointment with a consultant in London. On the morning of the appointment Sue was not feeling up to the three-hour drive so I decided it was time for the NHS to enter the modern world.

Attending the clinic on my own, the consultant announced her name. When I stood up and walked over the consultant looked confused.

"Sue's not well enough to attend but I have lined up a video call so you can speak to her at home." I said.

"I'm not sure how well that will work, said the consultant.

I told him I had travelled for three hours so it was worth a go.

We walked into his consulting room where I found two student doctors waiting for us.

"We'll be doing this appointment via video," he informed them as he sat down. "This is going to be more common in the future." He made it sound as if it was his idea in the first place.

Linking back home he then performed the consultation just as if Sue was in the room with one of the carers acting as a conduit for the conversation and even doing some basic movements of Sue's arms and legs. Sue had all the benefits of the session with none of the hassle, leaving me with the three-hour journey home.

Who would have predicted that his statement about appointments via video being "more common in the future" would become true so quickly, with coronavirus resulting in exactly that.

≈

In early December I performed the annual ritual of putting up the Christmas decorations. I really like the brightness that the decorations and lights bring into the house.

Over the years we have frequently succumbed to marketing hype and bought the latest, must have, 6ft artificial Christmas tree.

With a tree in every room our home was a tribute to the differing trends that existed through our 25 years of marriage.

We had the original traditional green one, a black tree (my favourite), a white tree, a green tree with snow on its leaves, then a tree with no leaves but ice and snow on the branches, and even a metal one.

Sue's favourite was a real tree – she loved the smell, so we headed to the local garden centre to choose one. She always knew exactly what she wanted and picking the tree was no different. The selection process was the same every year. I would end up pulling out every tree and holding it up, waiting for her to give the thumbs up or down, as if she were a Roman emperor in a coliseum. After an hour-long battle between me and the trees, we would return home triumphant, usually with the tree that I had suggested in the first place.

As Sue liked the smell and look of the real tree, we put it up in the room where she slept. I placed the baubles on the tree, and she would nod or make a noise to ensure that I placed every one of them in exactly the right spot. As always, she was in control, it looked stunning.

With the under-floor heating keeping the room at a constant warm temperature so she didn't feel cold it wasn't an ideal environment for a real tree to thrive. Undeterred Sue had one of the carers clamber under the tree every day to make sure the water was topped up.

To add to the ambience, I put lights outside. I wanted to create a winter wonderland in the back garden to help Sue's mood remain positive during the winter nights. I installed a herd of reindeer, put lights in the trees and ran garlands along the fence. The garden looked incredible.

As Christmas Eve arrived, we had the neighbours round for drinks and nibbles. The highlight was my favourite selfie of Sue, the neighbours and me all wearing Santa hats with massive smiles. We all looked so happy.

When we woke on Christmas Morning Santa Claus had visited as usual and left a stocking at the bottom of Sue's bed. Buying for someone who has a progressive, terminal illness is difficult as some of the usual gifts become less relevant or difficult to use, but it's not impossible and just requires more imagination. I, sorry I should have said Santa Claus, had filled the stocking with some perfume and a selection nail varnishes. Sue never lost her sense of smell and loved scented candles, so the stocking also had some of those. She loved watching the candlelight dancing across the walls.

Santa Claus gave me a backlit astro-photograph of Pickering's triangle. This is a star twenty times the size of our sun that exploded over 10,000 years ago. The photograph was taken from an observatory in the mountains of Nerpio, Spain. It took over two weeks to take the photograph and a lot of processing. When it is lit at night visitors always comment on the picture and spend ages just staring at the sheer number of stars. It's breath-taking.

We always had Christmas Day lunch on our own which was usually a fish curry. As Sue could not eat, she decided that she wanted to go out for a drive instead.

We searched for an open pub and ended up in The Tipsy Toad, a cocktail bar in Matlock. Unsurprisingly she had managed to find the only place that was full of young footballers. They made room for her whilst I sat on my own drinking a pint of shandy and eating a pack of salt and vinegar crisps. Some might argue it was the perfect Christmas Day lunch and I did enjoy the visit – but not as much as Sue.

Every family creates their own traditions and we were no exception. We always had lunch on our own and then hosted a Christmas Day evening buffet with party games for family and neighbours. Not letting MSA get in the way of this we rushed back from The Tipsy Toad and prepared for the evening's festivities that included the world's largest "pass the parcel". People always left with lots of little presents, none of which they needed or wanted but it was a lot of fun.

The "Godmother"

January 2019 to June 2019

Sue with Ilyana, our goddaughter, nestling in her arms. Ilyana was just 11 days old when this photo was taken on the 23rd of March 2019.

The "Godmother"

January 2019 to June 2019

On the 12th of March 2019 Ilyana was born to our close friends. Leading up to her birth we were honoured to be given a list of fifteen possible names. Sue ticked Ilyana which is an Arabic name and means "tender and delicate" or "kindness".

We met Ilyana for the first time when she was just three days old. Sue lay in her bed with Ilyana nestled in her arms. We were both asked to be godparents because of "our values" and "as role models". Despite Sue's illness and prognosis, they said that they could not think of anyone else that they would want to watch over Ilyana if the worst happened. It was a poignant moment.

Over the coming months a wonderful bond grew between Sue and Ilyana and I have some amazing memories and photos from the twelve months that they shared. When Sue passed away just after Ilyana's first birthday, I gave her one of Sue's cuddly tigers to keep. She has not let go of it since.

Whilst Sue is not here physically with Ilyana I know that she will be looking down on her and providing her with protection, love, support, and guidance. I also know that Sue will make sure that I fulfil our duty as godparents and that I live by the values that enable me to be a role model for Ilyana.

≈

In January Sue started to struggle with opening her eyelids. Our GP suggested we mention this to the neurologist who gave Botox injections for Sue's saliva glands. Sue had her first injection in January and it certainly helped although it did not eliminate the issue.

At the March MDT meeting we discussed how we had been increasing our use of out-of-hours GP and nursing care, so we completed a Right Care Management Plan. This ensures the continuity of care by clinicians who attend someone during the night. It provides information on the illness, symptoms and treatments being followed. This plan removed a lot of the anxiety and stress of dealing with clinicians who were meeting Sue for the first time late at night or in the early morning.

≈

During April I discovered that I could handle literally anything. I was in the middle of doing our Saturday morning shower routine when I dropped the sponge.

Crawling under the shower chair to reach it I suddenly felt something hit me on the back of the neck. Before I could react, I felt something else on my head and back.

Backing out from underneath the chair I had this sudden sinking feeling, and when I saw the mess around me, my worst fears were confirmed. Sue had had a very loose bowel movement and I had taken the brunt of it. Standing up I felt it run down my back and saw Sue smiling.

"Did you do that deliberately?" I asked.

Smiling even more, she simply nodded. I did not know whether to laugh or cry, so I did the former. It was not Sue's fault and there was no point getting angry, annoyed or frustrated, especially as I knew she had not really done this on purpose (well I do not think so).

I shouted to the carer for some help. Coincidentally it happened as the shift change for the carers was going on, so the outgoing carer handed me some gloves and a bag.

"I will leave that with you, John" she said as she walked out.

The incoming carer took one look. "I'm just going to check in and read the handover notes."

That left me standing there covered in, well you know…

The only option was to strip off and join Sue in having a shower.

Now, whenever somebody says, "the s#@t is about to hit the fan," I know exactly what that means. The memory still makes me smile.

≈

In early May we did our annual pilgrimage to Kedleston Hall to look at the bluebells. The walk around the grounds is beautiful. The bluebells form a magnificent blue scented carpet through the woodland. It is quite hilly and only partially wheelchair friendly but that did not stop Sue wanting to go. Perhaps she would have had a different perspective if it was her pushing the wheelchair. Suffice to say that I was tired by the time we had done the walk, but it made her happy, as bluebells were one of Sue’s favourite flowers and they reminded her of her Grandma.

In 1995 Sue had me transplant some of her Grandma’s bluebells into our first garden and we moved them again when we bought our home in 2007. Shortly after Sue passed away, I watched them flower in our garden. They seemed stronger and more beautiful as if they somehow knew what had happened and were showing their respects.

≈

One of the things that Sue enjoyed me doing was my “cookery masterclasses”. I would cook a meal but mimic the different personas of famous chefs. As the carers and Sue watched me act, they shook their heads in disbelief but always with a smile on their faces, and generally a lot of laughter.

I happily tried anything, never asking for help or advice on how to cook something I had never done before. Whilst most meals turned out all right there were a few that were inedible or looked strange.

The worst taste was an omelette where I put in way too much cheese. I then turned it over multiple times. By the time it was ready it looked like very greasy scrambled egg. Undeterred I took the first bite which was very cheesy but ok. By the fifth mouthful I realised that half a block of cheese might have been too much. Not prepared to accept that I couldn't cook an omelette I ate the whole thing and felt ill for the rest of the night.

The worst looking one was a poached egg. You might be asking what could possibly go wrong with that. Well, it appears quite a lot. Firstly, I had the saucepan on an intense boil. Then I just cracked two eggs into the water. The first egg spread across the water, with the second one separating. The saucepan looked like it was boiling milk as the egg whites frothed. Once I had managed to separate the eggs from the water, I placed them on the toast with the yolk of the separated egg looking like I had poached a ball of vanilla ice cream. I turned to Sue and the carers, presented my poached eggs on toast and announced that I had cooked a "deconstructed poached egg". I'm not sure that they believed me.

≈

In June I was invited to Royal Ascot. The dress code was a top hat and tails, so Sue helped me select the right outfit for the day.

The night before the event I collected the outfit on the way home. The hot pink tie and handkerchief Sue had chosen looked good and I felt rather dashing in the outfit.

I took the top hat off and put it onto the carer's head. The hat dropped down, covering her head and most of her neck. With her usual diplomatic style Sue simply burst out laughing.

After a quick change back into normal clothes I got in the car and drove to the hotel in Ascot. There I met up my three work colleagues. We agreed to meet in reception at 9am the following morning so we could get to Ascot Racecourse in plenty of time.

In the morning the gentlemen were ready at exactly 9am as instructed and then we sat in reception looking at our watches ticking past 9.15, 9.30 and even 9.45. Eventually the ladies came down at 10.00am. I was too much of a gentleman to point out that they were an hour late! Thankfully we had the Porsche, so we arrived in plenty of time.

Looking every bit the part as seasoned racegoers we arrived in our finery ready to make our millions.

Before every race I video called Sue and with the help of the carers she selected a horse. I then put the same size bet on her horse and the one I had chosen.

Over the five races Sue managed to choose more winners and placed horses than the four of us combined, resulting in a positive return on her bets. Her winning strategy was simply choosing her favourite horse's names and the colour of the jockey's jerseys that she liked, whilst I had studied the form. I will definitely adopt her strategy next time.

≈

Despite us trying to enjoy life as much as possible, we couldn't get away from the fact that the illness was catching up with Sue.

She had always preferred using the standing aid to transfer between the bed and either the wheelchair or the shower chair rather than using the hoist.

The problem was that standing aids should only be used for people who can load-bear through their legs, otherwise all of Sue's weight was taken from under her arms, which is unsafe.

We continued to use the standing aid for as long as we could but by June decided that we should switch to using the hoist as the only means of transfer for her safety and that of the carers. It was another sign of the illness progressing and I knew that Sue was unhappy with the decision but sometimes you just have to make the right decision no matter how unpalatable it may be.

Lady Parker

July 2019 to February 2020

Sue with Lady Parker in the nightclub

Lady Parker

July 2019 to February 2020

In July 2019 I left my previous company to start a new job in the airline industry. It was a strange thing to do given what was happening in our lives but an opportunity came up that I could not turn down and I was excited by the idea of a new challenge.

To celebrate I hired a nightclub venue and threw a party. I asked my personal assistant Rachel to be the DJ. She was a famous DJ known as "Lady Parker" in the early 2010's. She was based out of the Miss Moneypenny's nightclub in Birmingham. She has DJ'd in Moscow, Paris and Ibiza.

With over 200 guests including our parents, Sue's carers and my work colleagues we had a fantastic time. The party quickly turned into Sue's as everyone ignored me and focussed on making it a great night for her. We were still going strong at 2am before returning home in the Party Bus.

This was not the first, nor the last time that Sue and I went to a nightclub to watch Lady Parker perform. Sue loved music and enjoyed the atmosphere even if she couldn't dance. We went to see Lady Parker's comeback gig earlier in 2019 and Rachel had cleared an area next to her decks so that Sue could be close.

Another time watching Lady Parker spin her decks I saw a massive smile on Sue's face. Not sure what was happening I knelt by her side to ask. It was only then that I realised her head was at just the right height to watch the young male dancers gyrating on the dance floor. Everyone always made us welcome when we went into the nightclubs.

≈

I had the month of August off before starting my new job. We wanted to do a few day trips, but these were potential logistical nightmares due to Sue needing a hoist to use the toilet. Most people thought we were mad to attempt the trips, but we were determined.

I found a great website www.changing-places.org that lists all the disabled changing rooms with a full ceiling hoist, changing table and enough room. Using these locations, we were able to plot a journey that allowed us to visit Skegness, Twycross Zoo and Staines-Upon-Thames. Sue, the carer and I had a great time.

I bought disco lights that flashed in time with the music and we held parties with Sue, as usual, at the centre of it. By this time, she was generally in her bed but that did not stop her getting all dolled up and ready for action.

Occasionally she would fall asleep as the action rolled around her but for the most part she smiled as she listened to the flowing conversation or the antics of her Dad trying to dance at the bottom of her bed.

≈

During that month I also found a flat to rent in Staines-upon-Thames, so I had somewhere to stay when it was necessary for me to work down in London.

It was unfurnished so we had to buy some furniture. Sue wanted to make sure that I didn't feel too comfortable and would remember where home was, so she bought the cheapest sheets and duvet that she could find. Some duvets are advertised as being made "from feathers and down with no quills". I think she managed a duvet that was filled from all of those cut-off quills. Every time I got into bed all I could feel was the sharp points from the quills. It made me smile. I still haven't changed the duvet as the flat was, and never will be, home to me.

To stay in touch, I bought several Amazon Echo Shows which I installed in her bedroom, the flat, her parents, and my Mum and Dad's houses. This allowed Sue to dial into the flat to see whether I was there or not. I positioned it in the kitchen, dining room and lounge so that I could leave it on whilst I cooked, ate and watched TV. It really was like being in the room together and I was able to continue with my "cookery masterclasses".

Sue had always enjoyed watching Big Brother. The Amazon Echo Show allowed her to watch me as if I was a contestant, but I suspect that at times it was not that exciting, and it is just as well she could not vote to evict me on a Friday night.

≈

I mentioned earlier that Sue loved art and her favourite sculptor was Antony Gormley. You can imagine her disappointment when I was invited to a private viewing of his work at the Royal Academy of Arts on the 7th of November. She would normally have accompanied me but her MSA had progressed too much.

When I arrived, I explained to the hosts how much Sue loved Antony's work and asked if I could video call her as we walked around the exhibition. They were happy to oblige. I spent the whole tour looking through the phone as Sue enjoyed the view.

Her favourite exhibit was "Lost Horizon I" whilst mine was "Clearing VII". Unfortunately, I am not as refined as Sue so occasionally I had to stop myself laughing. In my defence, the beauty of art is that it is meant to trigger an emotional response.

≈

At Christmas we went to the Chatsworth House Christmas fair. Just like bluebell walk in Kedleston Hall, the Christmas fair is on a steep hill and not the easiest of places to push a wheelchair. Just as she had been on the bluebell pilgrimage, Sue was adamant that we would go.

It was only after some time of trying to push uphill, stop at each stall, start pushing, and weaving in and out of the crowd, that I realised it was much easier to push all the way to the top and then stop at each stall on the way back down.

As I said at the start of the book – Sue had the brains and I had admirably demonstrated that I was the just the brawn by nearly killing myself doing it the wrong way around.

At 2am on Christmas Day I was helping the carer do a pad change. I still do not know exactly how it happened but as we turned Sue her RIG tube popped out.

The carer did not know what to do but (fortunately) this was not the first time for me. Deflating the balloon, I carefully reinserted the tube whilst, in parallel, calling for an ambulance.

We found ourselves in A&E on Christmas Day at 4am. I think the A&E consultant was impressed by my medical knowledge of the action needed. The on-call enteral feeding nurse turned up at 8am to insert a new tube which took five minutes, then we waited until midday for a consultant to discharge us.

Rushing home, I got Sue back into bed followed by a frantic three hours getting the house and food ready for a Christmas party. That night twenty guests had been invited for the traditional Christmas buffet. They all turned up at 6pm blissfully unaware of how our Christmas Day had begun.

≈

In January and February 2020, we continued to do things together.

I would read magazines to Sue, showing her pictures of the latest celebrity to be caught in a compromising position.

We would listen to music, from the calm soothing music played at night to the latest UK top hits. I would sing along, replacing the words to make a unique song for her. We attempted to go to an outdoor music festival. It did not quite work out as the space for wheelchair users was too small and became crowded. With no shelter and the sun beating down Sue got too hot so we had to find shade but then she couldn't see the music acts, so we decided to leave. At least we had tried.

We did our Saturday morning ritual of shower, hair drying, and make-up before watching "Don't tell the bride" and "Say yes to the dress". I seriously cannot believe how many different episodes they recorded of these programmes. Sue and the carers would laugh as I commentated on some of the dresses – apparently, I could be quite brutal with my views. Strangely, I still watch them as it reminds me of those times with Sue.

We went to the cinema and watched the latest films. Sue's ability to tolerate stress was minimal so they would always be gentle films like Frozen 2 or Dr Doolittle.

One of our more regular trips was a visit to our local garden centre in Little Eaton which we did most weekends. Sue would always ensure she was smartly dressed, and the carer or I would wear a hole in the carpets bringing out one outfit after another as she decided which one she wanted to wear. I was always amazed how she could remember what clothes she owned.

Arriving at the garden centre looking as stunning as usual she always knew where she wanted to go and what plants she wanted to buy for me to plant later.

Exhausted, the carer and I would seek refreshments and rest in the garden centre cafe and we always ensured we bought some of Sue's feed along so that she could join in. We were often joined by our parents or my sister and her husband and there was always a lot of laughter. So much so that we soon became known to the staff, who were always so friendly towards Sue and were devastated when I told them she had passed away. It's amazing how Sue won over so many people's hearts.

Sue continued to shop on the internet using the carers to operate the iPad. I'm not sure who was encouraging who to buy what, but things kept appearing and disappearing with regularity. Apparently, they had got on first name terms with the Amazon delivery man (another young, good looking guy).

We continued to celebrate events like Valentine's Day. By now the carers were writing the cards for Sue and there would be a scribble where a carer had put a pen in Sue's hand and guided her signature. It can be difficult to choose a card for someone who is terminally ill as the words are not always appropriate.

On another occasion we hosted an anniversary party for her Mum and Dad. We asked them how they had met, and they shared the story. It was at a dance hall with a live band. Searching on Spotify I found three tunes. As I played them Sue's Mum and Dad danced around her bed. It was another amazing memory.

We have always operated an open-door policy and we didn't change that with the illness. Family, friends and neighbours came to visit us all the time and of course, our beautiful goddaughter visited regularly. The house was always full of life and Sue fed off this energy.

Sue would flirt with any young male that entered the house, especially if he had lovely, floppy hair. Given her condition it could be difficult to imagine her flirting but her smile and the twinkle in her eyes gave the game away every time.

Carers are meant to maintain an emotional distance from their clients to protect both the client and themselves but when looking after someone like Sue it is almost impossible. All the carers were so protective of her, treating her like a sister or daughter.

As Sue lost her independence and her ability to interact with the outside world diminished, I was determined that she would not end up just staring at the ceiling hence our drive to keep doing things. The carers were no different. They constantly found things to do creating what they called "magic moments".

The carers became part of our daily life. Sue became a trusted confidant as they shared their own stories to keep her spirits up and, as we heard more, they became like a family. This was not one way. Every carer who interacted with Sue said they had been enriched by the experience. They always said that although she had so many discomforts to deal with, she rarely complained and was fun to be around. They became emotionally attached to Sue, highly protective and massively loyal, and we were attached to them and often worried about what was going on in their lives.

I have said to so many of them that I am in their debt for looking after Sue and that I will always be there for them. It was not an idle promise but a genuine commitment.

And we continued to laugh. Sometimes at the illness, more frequently at the expense of the carers, but generally at me.

Our life was always hectic.

To give an example. In the first six months of 2018 we had 48 appointments with healthcare professionals either at home or at hospital. In parallel we had a further 10 appointments to keep everything running smoothly. We then had the usual daily influx of different carers (typically six per day) and community nurses visiting. Then there was all my work and business trips. And we were also trying to keep life as "normal" as possible, so we were also hosting birthday parties and going out.

To keep control and give Sue visibility we kept a desk diary of everything. Keeping a diary gave us things to look forward to and yet remain flexible enough to change those plans without feeling deflated or defeated. It also, with hindsight, has helped me to write this book and accurately reflect our journey.

The carers would often comment that we had a busier social life than they did. I think that it was this constant desire to keep doing things, to create a routine but also remain spontaneous, to enjoy life and make more memories, and to have a laugh no matter how bad things were, that helped us on our MSA journey.

A battle won

15th March 2020 to 22nd March 2020

Sue and I celebrating our 24th, and last, wedding anniversary together on the 9th of September 2019

A battle won

15th March 2020 to 22nd March 2020

On Sunday the 15th of March 2020 we went on our usual trip to the garden centre. Sue was in good form, smiling and, enjoying listening to the banter between her carer, my sister and myself.

In the afternoon our friend Dawn visited and bought Sue some flowers. She was the last person to do so.

If you had asked me how Sue was when I went into work on that Monday morning, I would have said she was doing well. I would never have guessed what would happen over the next two weeks.

Sue had some minor breathing issues on Tuesday morning. It was nothing dramatic, just struggling a bit. She was happy in herself.

We phoned the doctor and it was at this point that COVID-19 had begun to rear its head. The shortness of breath indicated it might be coronavirus, so the doctor would not come out. Instead they phoned for an ambulance, which quickly took Sue into hospital.

As I was at work it then developed into a race between me leaving work and them with blue lights flashing to see who would get to the hospital first.

The blue lights won. Sue was taken into A&E. It was chaos.

The hospital was just preparing for the coronavirus pandemic and had not got their response ready. Sue, along with eight other suspected cases, all arrived in the space of two hours. Sue was one of the first to arrive and kept apart from the non-COVID patients and was put into the resuscitation room. They quickly realised that they had blocked their major treatment room, so the next suspected coronavirus cases were put into the normal A&E department. Now they had blocked both facilities.

When I arrived, it was in meltdown. Worse still, they refused to allow me into the resuscitation room to see Sue in case I caught coronavirus.

I argued strongly that I should be permitted as Sue was unable to move her arms, speak and sometimes struggled to open her eyes. Like this she could not communicate with anyone and was probably scared. The A&E doctor would not budge, and security was called to remove me and the carers from the hospital.

I walked straight around the front and into the Patient Liaison Office, causing complete panic when I mentioned that my wife might have been admitted because of coronavirus. I demanded to see the hospital manager who arrived alongside the A&E manager. Both apologised and said that I should have been let in but been told to wear personal protection equipment (PPE).

In full PPE (gown, gloves, mask and visor) I arrived in A&E looking every bit the consultant. I was finally able to see Sue.

Oblivious to the stressful last hour I had endured, she was lying on the trolley, relaxed and more comfortable as a result of the oxygen. She laughed as soon as she saw me. Apparently, I did not look like a consultant at all but more like a clown. Yet again she had managed to see the funny side.

Sue was admitted into hospital on the coronavirus ward and a swab was taken. Relatives were not allowed to visit. Two very, very long days went by and then we had good news on Thursday night. It was not coronavirus, but a chest infection and I was asked to pick her up immediately. We returned home and got Sue comfortable in bed.

On Friday morning Sue started to regurgitate some of the feed. We were able to stop it easily by sitting her up, but I still called the doctor as it did not feel right. This time, with a negative coronavirus test result, the doctor came out and on seeing Sue was concerned so another ambulance was called.

Sue was admitted directly into the Surgical Assessment Unit, which was empty as all elective surgeries had been cancelled. After examining her, they organised some scans of her abdomen.

On Saturday morning at 1am the consultants broke the news that Sue had a blocked bowel and there was nothing they could do.

It was then that I made the hardest decision I have ever had to make and one that I never want to make again. I agreed with the consultants to stop the treatment of fluids and antibiotics and focus on making Sue comfortable, knowing that I had effectively made the decision to let Sue pass away.

That night was one of the longest of my life as I sat with the carer watching Sue as she slept. My mind raced as I tried to process what I had been told and what I knew was about to happen.

In the morning I phoned parents, siblings and friends to let them know what was happening. I am still not sure how I got through those conversations. Despite the fear of coronavirus, they wanted to see Sue to say "goodbye", so I arranged for people to come to see her at different times, so she was not overwhelmed.

I spent Saturday night in the room with Sue talking about all the things we had done together. The carer joined in with her memories of our journey.

On Sunday morning, the carers and nursing team stepped out of the room. Trying to be as strong as I could be, whilst being devastated inside, I told her what was happening. She simply smiled at me.

When the consultant came back into the room, she looked at him and gave him "that look". Even at the end she was still flirting.

Later that afternoon, on Sunday the 22nd of March at 6pm, Sue passed away peacefully with the sun shining through the window. She was pain free, relaxed and comfortable. One of the carers was holding her hand, Jan our Angel next door was holding her other hand, and I was in my usual place, at her feet.

Even though I knew that this time would come I was still not ready for the speed at the end, and nor was I prepared for it.

Sue's battle with MSA was finally over.

Through her inner strength; not letting her (or my) standards drop; a drive to continue to do our normal activities and live our fullest lives; an amazing sense of humour; and, a flirtatious interest in any young male, I believe we made the most of our journey with MSA.

Jan helped me gather Sue's things and I went home.

Walking into a dark, empty house for the first time without Sue and the noise of the carers reinforced the feeling of total loss. Not able to bear it I turned around and walked out. I had no idea what I was doing; I just wanted to get out.

Luckily Jan was just arriving back from the hospital. Seeing me on the doorstop she came into the house with me so I wouldn't be on my own. Her husband Eric joined us, and we raised a glass to toast my Sue and our memories of her.

Mum

22nd March 2020 to 29th March 2020

Mum preparing dinner whilst Sue and I share a joke

Mum

22nd March 2020 to 29th March 2020

It is at this point that coronavirus really enters the story. On Monday 23rd of March, the day after Sue passed away, the government announced lockdown in the UK and social distancing entered our vocabulary.

The normal grieving process was thrown out of the window. I found myself at home, on my own, with family and friends reaching out but not able to physically be present due to Covid-19 restrictions.

On Tuesday the 24th of March I started to do all the things you have to do when someone close to you dies. Everything was so much harder in a Covid-19 world. Organisations had sent their employees home and had increased levels of sickness. Everything had to be arranged on the internet or over the phone. As their call centres were struggling, everything took so much longer to resolve.

On Wednesday the 25th of March I spoke to my Mum and Dad. Mum was her usual comforting self, telling me it would be all right despite the fact she was feeling slightly unwell.

Friday the 27th of March was Mum's birthday. She was feeling better but very tired and it was strange not being able to be with her.

On the Sunday I received a call from my Dad that no son wants to hear – an ambulance crew were trying to resuscitate Mum. I immediately drove to their house and although it is just three miles away it felt like the longest drive ever.

I arrived to find Dad on the doorstep in tears, my sister sitting on a wall outside the house in the same state. I knew instantly that Mum had passed away. I was devastated.

In the space of one week I had lost both my wife and my Mum – two of the most important ladies in my life. I now found myself grieving and supporting my Dad with his grief at the same time.

Dad and I wouldn't have been able to get through this situation if it hadn't been for Karen, my amazing sister. She has always been my best friend. She made sure that we were both fine: running errands, ensuring we were eating and sleeping, and simply being there whilst having to come to terms with our grief and her own grief too.

Sue and Mum,

Two amazing women that I loved in different ways.

I miss you both so much

I know you are looking after each other

and keeping an eye on us.

A coronavirus world

29th March 2020 to November 2020

The two white horses with blue plumes

A coronavirus world

29th March 2020 to November 2020

Organising funerals and sorting out the details in a coronavirus world of lockdown and social distancing was strange.

Sue and Mum loved flowers, but all the florists were shut. I tried all sorts of avenues and eventually, through a friend of a friend, managed to find a florist that was now working from her garage and I ordered some beautiful flowers arranged to spell the words "Tiger" and "Mum". It felt right to put the toy rat, that Jan had bought Sue to help with her finger clenching, into the coffin, as it had given Sue so much comfort over the last eighteen months.

Organising the funeral was equally difficult. Churches were closed, a cremation was the only option. I could have had a hearse, but social distancing prevented cars for mourners, so we had to drive ourselves. There were only eight mourners allowed and rigid rules on how to behave: no hugging and no approaching the coffin. There were even restrictions on how the coffin could be moved with no pall bearers. And as everywhere was in lockdown a wake was not possible.

On the 14th of April a horse drawn hearse with two white horses decked out in blue (Sue's favourite colour) left our house. Our neighbours stood at the end of their drives and waved Sue off. It was a moving tribute.

I had not realised how slowly horses walk. An hour later we arrived at the crematorium. We would have caused chaos on the A6 if it had not been for the lack of traffic due to coronavirus.

Walking into the crematorium we had to sit in suitably distanced chairs. It just did not feel right, so we all moved our chairs together, dragging them noisily on the floor. We then realised that we were too far away from the celebrant and had to drag ourselves back towards her. The first thing she said was "Thank you for maintaining your social distance" making us all laugh. It was inappropriate humour again breaking through the sadness we all felt.

I wanted to get the music right. As we entered the crematorium, a "Night full of stars" by Coldplay was played, which was Sue's favourite song. We both loved Kylie Minogue and "I want to go out dancing" seemed the perfect tune to play as we left, making us all smile.

I received over sixty sympathy cards for Sue but one in particular is my "favourite". Mia, the daughter of close friends, created a homemade card with a sunflower on it, which was one of Sue's favourite flowers. She used a lolly pop stick for the stem, green rubber for leaves, scrunched up yellow tissue paper for the petals, and a little red pom pom for the centre of the sunflower. She had painted the grass and sky, so it stood out. She had written inside that she would "miss Sue very much" and signed it using a felt tip pen with different coloured kisses. It was a beautiful card and it summed up how everyone felt.

Four days later we repeated the Covid-funeral experience for my Mum.

3 letters, 3 promises, 1 card

Unknown to me Sue had written three letters at different times in the illness. I found them as I started to tidy things up after the funeral. The courage she had demonstrated throughout the illness now came through in the words she had written.

The first letter was written in May 2015 and it is difficult to know exactly when she wrote the other two, as there were no dates on them, but the deteriorating handwriting indicates the approximate times.

First letter

This letter was written just before we went back to the consultant. She wrote about knowing in her heart what the consultant was going to say. She asked for forgiveness for the impact that her illnesses had had on our life together and what she was about to put us through as a result of the diagnosis.

I just hope that by the end of the illness she knew she had never needed to ask for forgiveness. It was amazing to be Sue's soulmate and have her as part of my life.

The illness made us stronger as a couple and reinforced my feelings for her repeatedly. Whilst I would never want her or anyone else to suffer MSA I know that it made me realise how lucky I was to have had her in my life.

Second letter

The second letter was like a performance review that I would have at work. She described the life she had with me and how she had felt throughout. She highlighted the things that she loved and admired about me. She had had no regrets and talked of our special relationship.

I know for sure that she knew I loved and admired her. On the Saturday before she passed away, I was able to tell her all the things I had loved about her.

The letter also told me to look after myself; to rest and relax, to eat properly, to exercise, and to get a balance between work and life. I have tried hard to do these things.

Third letter

This letter was hardest to read and not just because her handwriting had deteriorated.

She wrote about me not carrying forward the burden of pain that she had caused throughout the illness. I don't really understand what she meant by this sentence. I wish that I could talk to her about it and reassure her that it was never a burden. It was a huge privilege to have looked after her.

She talked about tidying the house and used the terms "getting rid of the chaos I caused" and "only keep one or two items if necessary".

It's true to say that things were chaotic at times but that was part of us trying to continue to live our lives to the full. I have found it impossible to "just keep one or two items" and having them around the house is comforting.

Her final points were about moving on in life. I am not sure how I am meant to do that as she was, and still is, a massive part of who I am.

One card

With the letters there was also a Star Wars themed Valentine's card. The card had a printed message in it. I don't know whether Sue had bought it for the Valentine's Day just before she passed away and had forgotten to give it to me (which is unlikely as she had a fantastic memory) or whether she got it for me to look at on future Valentine's Days. Either way I will treasure it, remember the love we shared, and never forget the depth of feelings we had for each other.

Three promises

I promised myself over the last seven years that Sue's battle would not be for nothing nor forgotten.

I am not sure what I meant by this promise, but it has been the motivator to create a photobook that celebrates Sue's life. I have given a copy of it to many of our family and friends. It has also driven me to write the story of our journey with MSA to raise awareness, provide insight into how we coped and hopefully to help others.

Sue asked me to make three promises to her during her illness. I have never broken a promise to her, so I am determined to keep them.

Promise 1: I would get fit and lose weight

Having prioritised Sue's care, I stopped exercising and gained weight, which I know frustrated her.

A friend sponsored me £100 to hit my initial target of losing three stone in weight, which I managed in the first three months after Sue passed away.

More friends sponsored me to lose a further two stones. I managed to surpass that target in mid-November 2020 bringing the weight loss to five stone in total.

With my friends support we raised over £500, which was donated to the UK MSA Trust. With other activities and donations, we raised over £10,000 in Sue's memory.

Promise 2: I would not dwell on the past nor what happened during the illness

I understood what Sue was trying to say but I have more positive memories from our battle with MSA than negative ones.

We kept doing things that we did before but also things we would never have done, had it not been for MSA. We had fun and a lot of laughter. We generated so many happy memories that I cherish. And we formed new friendships including with the carers, with whom I am still in touch.

Promise 3: I would move on and live, as she called it, "the next third of my life"

Again, I understood what Sue was trying to say but I found this promise difficult to make. She was keen that I should be happy and enjoy the rest of my life. I think this gave her some comfort but making this promise felt like I was abandoning her before she had passed away.

Perhaps, in the fullness of time, meeting this promise may be possible but as I write this chapter, I am uncertain how and when that will be.

Acknowledging my losses…

I have come to the realisation that everybody grieves in a different way and we all come to grief from different places.

Even though we have all lost the same person, we all had a different relationship with Sue. I lost my wife but for others they have lost their daughter, sister, godmother, (best) friend, neighbour, client or patient. These labels can mean so many different things.

Sue was not just my wife. She was my soulmate, my lover, my best friend, my confidant, my purpose, my everything. We had been together for over 30 years and shared so much.

The relationship combined with the circumstances, and many other factors, made the grieving process, timeline and experience such a personal and unique thing. I believe there is no right or wrong way to deal with it.

After eight months I was still in the process of grieving.

There was not an hour that went by where I did not think about her. Some days were extremely difficult. I felt a profound sense of loss and loneliness, especially at the weekends, and I struggled to explain those feelings.

I was surprised by how lonely I felt. I have a loving family, group of friends and work colleagues who provided me with support throughout the journey and given me so much of their precious time. I have a wide variety of interests: sport; gardening; films and box sets; reading; walking and cooking. And whilst I really enjoy being with people and just being able to talk, I have always been someone who has been "comfortable with their own company".

It took me time to realise why I felt that loss so deeply. Sue had shaped who I was and I, similarly, had shaped who she was. Our identities were intertwined.

She was the person I woke up with every morning. She was the first and last person I spoke to in every one of the 10,950 days we were together. We knew what the other was thinking and feeling without the need to speak. A simple look could convey a whole conversation.

We had our routines. I made her tea and toast every morning, which she had in bed. We had the same interests and the same sense of humour (mine is probably a bit more guttural). We had built a history with shared memories that were only ours to keep.

She was the person I turned to for advice. I trusted her implicitly. She always had my interests at heart. If I was worried, she was always able to put me at ease. We had dreams and goals, things we would do together in the future.

Then she was gone.

At home I had been used to her continual presence, along with the noise and activity of the carers. The first time I walked into the dark, empty house after Sue passed away, there was a feeling of total loss.

It was later that night after Jan and Eric had left that I felt the profound sense of loneliness for the first time.

I realised that I would never hear Sue's voice again or her laughter. I would never be able to hold, hug or kiss her. I would not feel the warmth of her skin or the softness of her hair in my fingers. I found myself holding an item of clothing just so I could smell her scent again. I would not be able to tell (or bore) her about my day or my worries, nor seek her guidance or reassurance.

I even found myself missing the routines and chaos that had become the norm as a result of MSA. The lockdown prevented companies and charities from collecting the equipment we had used so there were constant reminders of the journey we had undertaken. I would find myself standing at the foot of the bed where she had slept just staring.

Knowing that Sue would eventually pass away did not make it any easier nor did it prepare me any better. The gap in my life was still the same.

When Mum passed away a week later another massive gap opened in my life. The suddenness and shock hit me so hard that I was devastated. I could not process it and just felt numb. The last time I had seen her was the night before Sue passed away. She had hugged me and said it would be ok. The last time I spoke to her was to wish her happy birthday.

With two massive gaps I made myself busy arranging the funerals and organising all the stuff that must be sorted out after someone passes away.

Coronavirus reared its head again as it ravaged the airline industry, so I returned to work in the office straight away to help lead our response to the pandemic. It felt right to keep busy and gave me something to focus on. However, the experience was different from usual. The majority of people were working remotely, so I only saw them on the computer screen, but it did get me out of the house during the week.

I also tried to keep myself busy tidying up the house. It was a couple of months before I was ready to take Sue's things to the charity shop, but this was delayed further as a result of the lockdown. I folded every piece of clothing carefully savouring the memories of when we had bought them, the times she had worn them and what we had been doing. I have kept some of my favourite things and look at them frequently.

I realised after about three months that I had not given myself the space and time to acknowledge what had happened and to start grieving properly. I had tried to fill the gaps left by Sue and Mum by keeping myself busy and returning to work too quickly.

I started to talk through my memories, thoughts and feelings with my family and friends. The grief for my Mum really hit me when we had interred her ashes. I realised that I had not grieved for her properly. She had passed away a week after Sue, so I was still dealing with losing Sue. We then cremated Mum the same week as Sue, so I was, again, dealing with both at the same time. When we interred Mum there was only that to think about and in the days leading up to it the grief rolled over me in waves.

I was finally acknowledging my losses.

I eventually realised that I needed to find a different balance to my life; to give myself the approval to develop new and different relationships; to experience new things and start making new memories that Sue would not be part of. The emptiness may always be there but over time these new things will grow, and the gap may not feel so large or dominate as much.

I have an increasing number of days where I feel stronger and more positive. The future contains more opportunities even though taking them feels scary.

Even after twelve months there are still days when the thin veneer of being "ok" is punctured by someone saying or doing something kind and the grief becomes visible. I felt guilty when this first happened, but I have now realised that it is normal and healthy.

I do think that as a society we sometimes struggle with grief and I was surprised by a few people who remained largely absent through the whole process. Perhaps it was their own way of coping with grief or not knowing what to do or say, however I tried not to judge them for being absent when I needed them the most.

On the flip side, I was equally surprised how some of my friends really were there to embrace this difficult time.

Many of my friends navigated their way through social distancing, shielding and the constant changing of rules around lockdown and tiering to provide me with a huge amount of support in spite of the other things happening in their lives.

Some of them took me out for meals, joined me on a walk, organised picnics, ordered takeaways or sat in the garden having a socially-distanced coffee. During the three lockdowns I was supported through virtual drinks, parties, quiz nights, and time talking on the phone.

My closest and dearest friends pulled me even closer to their families. They became a bigger part of my life, helping me to move towards that new balance. They spent more time with me than I could have expected. We talked for hours sharing our memories about Sue. They will never fully understand how much they have helped me navigate the last twelve months without my soulmate by my side.

It can be the case that we need to support people through grief when we are grieving ourselves. I am not sure if there is a right or wrong way to help someone through grief. But if you do find yourself able to support someone, the following suggestions are based on what helped me. They might also give you ideas how to ask for help and support for yourself.

- Reach out and offer to talk whenever the grieving person needs you.

- Stay in touch after the initial few weeks – this is when the real sense of loss and loneliness can strike, especially if the grieving person lives on their own.

- Prepare a meal, a cake or biscuits – it is a cliché, but it means a lot.

- Invite the grieving person round for a drink, cook a meal or go for a walk with them. I really appreciated the company and it gave a focus to look forward to.

- Offer to do something specific for the grieving person rather than a more generic offer of help, e.g. I will get you some food shopping.

- Let the grieving person talk in order to share memories.

- Do not let the fear of someone showing grief, or not knowing what to say, stop you from saying or doing something.

- The journey that the grieving person is undergoing is personal. Do not use platitudes or set false expectations. Try not to compare but do share your own experiences. I found that there was no agreed way to feel, no set process to follow or timeline to beat. It is best not to judge, just reassure them that what they are feeling is okay and you will be there for them.

- Finally, if you can, give them a hug – it made me feel better every time.

Some of my friends said to me that it must have been harder to grieve for Sue and Mum in a coronavirus-dominated world. This is impossible to answer.

Having small funerals allowed me to focus on Sue, Mum and my memories. I did not feel that I was being watched and could let my grief out freely. On the other hand, I know that there were so many people who wanted to support us and be able also to say their goodbyes, but they were unable to attend due to lockdown rules.

Whilst we were able to arrange the cremation, we were not able to arrange the interment of Sue's ashes, as churches and cemeteries were closed. I also wanted to wait for a time to allow as many people as possible to attend.

The lack of being able to have a wake prevented us meeting each other after the cremation and share our memories. Like so many people who lost loved ones during the coronavirus pandemic, I decided to schedule a party to celebrate Sue's life in early 2021 but further restrictions have resulted in more delays so this will now happen over twelve months after she passed away.

Normally people would come and visit but the initial lockdown, then the introduction of Covid-19 local restriction tiers followed by a second (and third) lockdown meant that many people were prevented from visiting.

When Sue was first diagnosed, I talked to my boss about whether to give up work, even though I could not afford to. He said that, in his experience, when going through a crisis in life you need an area of stability and work would provide that. He was right as it provided me with structure, a daily routine and plenty of distraction from the challenges of caring for Sue. However, we could not have anticipated the impact of coronavirus on working life. As part of the management committee of an airline group severely affected by the global pandemic, the challenge and pressure we faced was enormous. I had to respond whilst I also came to terms with my grief, which, in itself, was impacted by the closure of the offices. I had lost my normal support networks that exist in the workplace.

The positives that have come out of the coronavirus pandemic include the fact that I was able to give up my unhealthy eating habits and gave me the opportunity to get fit as well as having the time to reflect in private.

Tiger

My favourite picture of Sue – she loved her tea.
This was taken at Widecombe Fair in Devon.
12th of September 2006

Tiger

Sue was the most amazing person I have ever met. She was a beautiful person inside and out. She was warm, loving and kind. She always had time for people and made them feel special.

Her courage, spirit and determination came to the fore whatever life threw at her. These challenges were multiple including Crohn's disease, endometriosis and multiple system atrophy.

She had an amazing sense of style. Her eye for colour was astonishing, evidenced when we bought my car. People often assumed we had used an interior designer for our home.

When we were dating, she was part of a dramatics society (she was a great actress). I could never remember the lines, so I was relegated to "behind the scenes" making the scenery.

She was a fantastic teacher loved by children, parents and teachers alike and was an inspiration to all of them and whoever she met.

She had an amazing sense of humour, which came to the surface when she was relaxed with people. She also had a "naughty streak" and would be more than happy to cause mischief or play a prank. She loved music and dancing.

She was open and honest, with an incredible ability to assess a person and their character in a very, very short time. Maybe it was the Psychology degree or just a sixth sense but the blend of these two things got us into problems a couple of times.

One story springs to mind. I remember having a friend over for dinner with his new girlfriend. The conversation was a bit stilted. I asked my favourite conversation breaker: "If you had a tattoo what would it be?" Sue said a flower, my friend a landscape, and I said an eagle. We waited for the girlfriends reply. As she thought for a few seconds, Sue blurted out, "snake in the grass!" Not really a term of endearment. I quickly thought of a lame reason as to why Sue had said that, but the meal didn't last much longer and nor did the relationship. Sue had, again, understood a person and got their personality spot on.

Sue was also very intelligent. She was a straight A student at school and achieved a first in her degree (despite being affected by poor health throughout her educational years).

She had the most beautiful smile that was endearing and disarming in equal measure.

My nickname for her was Tiger. She was definitely cute and cuddly but could have her moments, especially if someone threatened her family or friends. Then, as I described those rare moments, the tail would swish, the teeth were bared and the claws came out. Her nickname for me was Gorilla, a "gentle giant with a silver back".

The 17th of June 2020 would have been Sue's 50th birthday. She was so close to making this major milestone. I still bought her a card and wrote in it how much she means to me. I signed it as I always did….

With all my love
Now and forever
Gorilla xxx

We had an online party to celebrate with friends and family and toasted her memory. The 9th of September 2020 would have been our 25th wedding anniversary.

They broke the mould when Sue was born. She was a special person and holds a special place in many people's hearts. She will remain an inspiration and continue to be missed by all who knew her.

The following pages have some of my favourite photographs of Sue, which will hopefully give a bit more insight into her life…

Celebrating her 37th birthday in the Santuari de Lluc monastery, north-west Majorca.

We stayed in the Belmond, La Residencia in Deia.

The picture always brings back memories of the many happy holidays we had together in Salcombe, Devon. This was on her 44th birthday, the last time we visited.

We would catch the ferry (a small boat) to Sunny Cove and have picnics on the beach. It is one of my favourite places to visit.

Duffield Carnival, an annual event held in June with stalls, events, displays, the Women's Institute baking competitions (always keenly contested), BBQ's, ice cream vans, live music and beer tent.

Venetian Ball on the Queen Elizabeth cruise ship as we sailed from Southampton, UK to New York, USA in October 2011 for a business trip.

For our 14th wedding anniversary in September 2009 I took Sue to the Trentham Monkey Forest in Stoke-On-Trent.

I was often asked by friends and carers how I met Sue?

Sue was my younger sister's best friend at school. Sue lived a few streets from the school and she and my sister would turn up to afternoon registration and then "bunk off" lessons that did not interest them. They would go to Sue's house, claiming to watch News at One, although I always said that they were really watching Rainbow and other kids' TV programmes. Unfortunately, they did this too often which resulted in many detentions.

Whilst I was aware of Sue it was not until she was 15 that I became interested. My sister finally succumbed to my pressure and arranged a date between Sue and myself. We went out for a meal, which was very nice, but the "date" was a bit of a disaster. The feedback that Sue gave my sister was not exactly the best reference I have ever been given but probably accurately reflected the teenage boy I was. Undeterred I managed to persuade Sue to give me another chance and the second date simply reinforced her opinion, so we did not speak for another three years.

In July 1990 my sister married my best friend. There is a whole different story about how that relationship developed but the summary is that he worked with me at WHSmith's as a Saturday assistant. We would go to each other's house on a Saturday night to spend our hard-earned wages on watching back-to-back horror movies from Blockbusters – you had to visit a shop and pay to rent a video in those days.

It was after about eighteen months that I finally realised I was watching these on my own. I had no idea why he was spending more time with my sister upstairs than watching the horror movies with me downstairs.

Sue was a bridesmaid and I was an usher at my sister's wedding. Sue looked gorgeous so I asked her out for the third time. Playing hard to get she said no and ended up going out with someone else at the wedding.

By now I had graduated from Staffordshire Polytechnic and joined Rolls-Royce. In 1992 Sue had major abdominal surgery for her Crohn's disease. My sister decided to visit Sue as she recovered at home and asked if I could go with her. Feeling the need to bring a present I bought a cuddly toy – it was a 6ft rabbit which seemed like a great idea at the time.

Arriving at Sue's house we found her lying on the sofa, clearly in discomfort. She had only just been discharged and I still do not know what came over me, but I asked her out again.

Clearly shocked she said, "No, I've only just got out of hospital."

Interestingly I took this as a "Maybe, just not tonight".

I then phoned her every Friday asking how she was and whether she was ready to go out yet. To my shock and delight she eventually said "yes" after about eight weeks. What I didn't realise was that her Dad had said, "For god's sake, just say yes so he stops ringing on a Friday night."

The date night finally arrived, and we went out to a local pub. To Sue's surprise she enjoyed it, so we started dating, going out every Wednesday and Friday night. We taught each other many things but the main one I can talk about is that she learnt how to play pool.

Our romance continued to blossom, and we saw more and more of each other. We then had our first holiday away together. As we still both lived with our parents this was a big deal as it would be the first time, we had spent a long time together. We rented a cheap cottage in Devon arriving to find that it needed "deep cleaning" and spent the first three hours doing so.

Upon waking I heard Sue's mum and dad's voices coming from the kitchen. Walking in I found three faces frowning at me and it did not help when I laughed as they explained what had happened.

After falling asleep that night Sue had had problems breathing due to the feather pillows (some allergic reaction). She had tried to wake me up, but I had made some uninterested noises and gone back to sleep.

Upset and unable to sleep Sue had got up. Wanting to talk to her mum and dad about what had happened and my "uncaring" response. As there was no phone in the cottage (this was way before we had mobiles) she decided to walk to the nearest village and find a phone box.

Wearing a nightdress and dressing gown she had walked out of the cottage but was unaware that the garden was two tiered. She had fallen down a ledge and cut her knees. In tears, she had then wandered a mile into the village and called her mum and dad at 2am in the morning. They immediately packed some pillows and driven four hours down to Devon, arriving at 7am to comfort her. I woke at 8am oblivious to the whole saga.

I can admit that this was not my finest hour.

Sue's mum and dad joined us for the rest of the holiday, and we repeated "our" annual holiday with them in Devon for the next fifteen years.

Over the next 18 months Sue and I grew closer together. Still living with our parents, we would often go away for a weekend.

In September 1994 we stayed in a lovely country hotel. After dinner we retired to the lounge. The room was lit by candlelight and a roaring log fire with soft music playing. To this day I still don't know what caused me to do it. I hadn't thought about it before the weekend, I hadn't planned it, and I didn't have a ring, but I found myself on one knee proposing marriage.

The silence was deafening. She didn't respond positively or negatively. In fact, she didn't say anything – she simply stared at me as if I had spoken a foreign language.

"Er, perhaps we should go to bed," I said, after what seemed like a very, very long silence.

She didn't say anything about my proposal for the rest of the weekend.

When I got home my mum and dad asked how the trip had gone. In a very British way, I replied "interesting" and moved the conversation on to a different topic before I had to recount the humiliation of proposing and getting no response.

Six months later, when sitting in Carsington Reservoir cafe having a cup of tea out of plastic cups, Sue, out of the blue, said, "You haven't asked me the question again?"

Being a "typical bloke" I thought she was referring to me not asking her whether she wanted sugar in her tea. Correcting my misunderstanding she said, "You know, what you said in September."

I found myself down on one knee for the second time proposing. This time she said "Yes", much to my relief and the delight of all those people sitting around us. I never asked her why it took her six months to think about my proposal.

We drove up to Sheffield to look at engagement rings. I found myself entering a world that I knew nothing about. I thought that all rings were the same but learnt rapidly about clarity, colour, carat and cut. We settled on a gold solitaire engagement ring with six prongs holding in the diamond. We agreed that we would make our engagement formal on the 14th of February and would collect the ring the weekend before.

I finished work early on Friday, drove to Sheffield to collect the ring, managing to return to Derby by 6pm to play five-a-side football. I was paranoid about losing the ring, so I placed it behind the goal to keep an eye on it, consequently suffering an hour of humiliation from my friends making fun of me.

With the ring burning a hole in my pocket, I drove to Sue's house so that I could surprise her. Normally her mum and dad would go upstairs around 9pm. This time her mum decided to stay downstairs and at midnight said, "Isn't it time for you to go, John?".

With the ring still in the pocket I thought I was going to miss the chance to surprise Sue. Fortunately, her Mum left the room. I quickly went down on one knee for the third time now holding the ring in my outstretched hand.

Sue squealed. Her Mum rushed back in to see what was happening and called Sue's dad downstairs. Asking for his permission to marry Sue, he bizarrely just stared at me and said nothing.

It was the first real insight I had that Sue and her dad were so alike. I saw it repeatedly throughout our twenty-five years of marriage.

We set the date of the wedding for the 9th of September 1995 and decided to have our honeymoon in May as it was cheaper. On the 20th of May we arrived in Carvoeiro, Portugal for two weeks with Sue's mum and dad joining us. I think it was their way of ensuring the pillow situation on our first holiday did not repeat itself.

It was only after we got married that I found out that Sue was not really bothered about cuddly toys. The fact that I had bought her a 6ft rabbit when she was ill had not gone down well. She was determined to throw it out, but I never allowed her to as it was the first present I had bought her. The compromise was that it was wrapped in a black bag and stuck in the loft. Looking back at the dawn raid by the police it is just as well they did not search the house. I am not sure what they would have thought if they had found a black bag with what looked like a body in it.

My reflections

At some point in our lives we may know someone who is looking after a partner with a serious illness and have a degree of sympathy with them, especially if the illness is terminal and progressive. It is only now, though, that I truly understand what it is like to live with someone who has a progressive illness.

MSA totally dominated and changed our lives in every aspect. It started before the diagnosis, throughout the illness, and afterwards. It affected not only Sue and myself, but everyone around us.

Sue and my relationship changed as the illness progressed and she became increasingly dependent on me.

Whilst Sue battled with the physical and emotional changes happening to her, I had to transition into the role of primary carer. I did not apply for the role. I did not have any qualifications, nor did I have any experience and there was little, if any, training provided.

I threw myself into the challenge of being the primary carer whilst also having to come to terms with the physical and emotional impact on Sue and myself.

There would be days that I was exhausted, nearly falling asleep in meetings or on the way to and from work. Whilst others could rest after work or at the weekend, I would have to switch focus and become the primary carer. I never stopped to gather my breath.

I never anticipated the challenges that I would face, how I would overcome them, and what I would be able to do.

I have continually surprised myself at what I can cope with but there is nothing special about me. I am just a normal guy who fell in love and married a wonderful and special lady.

Looking back over the journey, my top ten pieces of advice would be:

- **Never beat yourself up for what you cannot do and the mistakes you make.** It does not matter if you….

    - cannot be the primary carer
    - cannot be involved in the care activities
    - are unable or unwilling to do something
    - are unhappy to do something
    - make mistakes when doing something

  Instead, my advice would be to **focus on what you can do. Be at peace with yourself and happy knowing that you are doing your best for the person you love.**

- If you want to be the primary carer or provide the care at home for as long as possible, then do not worry. **If I can become a primary carer then anyone can**. I got involved, tried my best and I never gave up. I asked questions and learnt on the way. Occasionally I didn't get it quite right, but I learnt from those moments and moved forwards.

- **Focus on what you can change, not what you cannot.** Very early on I accepted the diagnosis and the eventual outcome even though I prayed that it would not happen. However, I put all my energy and focus on making the journey as good as it could be. I knew that I could make the journey easier for Sue and turn it into a positive rather than a negative experience. We achieved this.

- **Discuss and make any big decisions early on.** Sue's ability to communicate her thoughts and wishes diminished as the illness progressed. It became slower, harder and more tiring for her during late 2017 and almost impossible by the end of 2018. We had four key discussions in 2016:

    - where we would provide Sue's care, i.e. at home or a care home

    - how and who would provide Sue's care

    - what would happen if she needed emergency care and treatment, i.e. the NHS ReSPECT form

  - what would happen at the end of her battle, i.e. palliative care and funeral arrangements

  Discussing these in advance meant that at the critical times some of the pressure was relieved; I knew what Sue wanted and I was able to fulfil her wishes.

- **Try to get ahead of the illness.** Unfortunately, MSA progresses very quickly at times but there are also periods of stability. Planning ahead and making adaptations early meant that when the illness did progress, we were ready. Examples include providing toilet risers, grab handles, stair lift, ramp into the house and a profiling bed.

- **Do not be afraid to ask for help, either physically, emotionally or financially.** This is not a sign of weakness or failure but a confident and strong statement. It is simply a recognition that it is impossible to do everything yourself. There are many areas that help can come from: family; friends; neighbours; work colleagues; GPs and other healthcare professionals; social services; care workers; respite care and hospices; churches and charities.

- **Persistence, resilience and determination is needed**, for example when seeking funding. The system is set up to optimise the allocation of constrained funds. You need to fight to get the right level of care, especially given the limited understanding of the illness.

- **Talk openly about what is happening and how you feel.** This can be an important coping mechanism although it was not easy for me.

  One of the more important conversations I had was with my work so they could understand what was happening and were therefore supportive when I needed to prioritise Sue, for example, to attend appointments.

- **Put in place a lasting power of attorney (LPA).** This helped me to implement Sue's wishes from a health and financial perspective when communication became more difficult for her.

- **Make time for, and look after yourself.** I wanted to ensure the care provided was excellent. I had always looked after Sue so wanted to be personally involved as much as possible. I achieved both of those things but in doing so I de-prioritised my own health. I was exhausted at times. I gained a lot of weight. If I took a break, I felt guilty. My friends tried to tell me to look after myself, but I ignored them. It is only now looking back I realise they were right.

I think that this experience has changed me as a person.

I have learnt so much in ways that I did not expect. For example, I think that the whole experience has made me a better business leader as I now have more patience and empathy.

My final reflection is that we made the best of a terrible and cruel situation. **It made us even stronger as a couple.** The outcome was inevitable. The journey was not, and I would not change anything we did.

With thanks

Jan, our angel next door, with Sue

With thanks

...to my amazing family, friends and work colleagues...

The support of family, friends and work colleagues was critical. It would have been impossible to face MSA without your help. I cannot mention you by name as I do not want to upset anyone by missing them out. What I do know though is that you know who you are and what you did for us. I cried with you, I laughed with you, I let off steam with you, I went for walks with you, I sat in silence with you, and I talked through what was happening. You were always there for me.

Without you this story would be so different. I would not have been able to have provided the support Sue needed. Because of you, Sue and I made so many more memories that I now cherish. With your help, we had lots of laughter along the way, and we managed to make the journey with MSA as good as it could be.

I would also like to give a special thanks to all of you who have encouraged me to write this book and had the courage to tell me how to improve it.

A special thank you to my friend and editor whose insights and comments have helped me to create something that will keep Sue's memory alive forever and will help others on the MSA journey. Also, thanks to a friend at work for her expertise in steering me towards a front cover that truly reflected Sue and I being soulmates.

...to our neighbours and great friends...

When Sue passed away Jan and Eric were there, ensuring that I was ok. I am also blessed with other amazing neighbours; Jo and Mark, Ann and Chris, and Eileen and Douglas, although the home-made ginger nuts, cakes and meals did not help my diet.

...to the most compassionate carers...

Throughout the journey we were supported by an excellent team of daytime carers and personal assistants from Bluebird Care (Belper) and Right at Home (Derby); and the night-time carers from AMG Healthcare (Chesterfield).

There were so many carers who were involved and came into our home to support Sue. A massive thank you to the small army of over 78 day-time carers including:

Abbie, Ange, Angel, Angela, Angie, Annie, Ashleigh, Barbara, Bev, Bex, Bojanna, Carla, Caroline, Cheril, Danielle, Deborah, Elizabeth, Emily, Emma, Esther, Gemma, Gillian, Giorgia, Hannah, Hayley, Helen, Helena, Jackie, Jade, Jane, Jayne, Jennifer, Jess, Jessica, Julie, Joanna, Jody, Josie, Karen, Katie, Kelly, Kerry, Kirsty, Lauren, Leanne, Lesley, Linda, Liz, Lorayne, Lorna, Louise, Lynn, Marina, Mia, Michelle, Natalie, Nikita, Nirmal, Racheal, Rebecca, Rhiannon, Rio, Ruth, Paige, Sara, Sarah, Shannon, Sharon, Sharron, Shirley, Shirlena, Siobahn, Sue, Susan, Tracey, Trina, Vicky, and Wendy.

Our first day-time carer entered our lives on Monday 3rd of August 2015. That week we had one hour of care per day on four days to help Sue prepare her lunch. Our longest serving carer was Jayne who was with us for four and a half years. Every carer had a different set of skills and personality. Jayne was calm and provided continuity as new carers came and went. Thanks, also, to the carer who wrote a lovely note letting me know what a great job I was doing. At that time, it was just what I needed to hear.

I have already mentioned the night time team, but my thanks again to Aana, Amanda, Amy, Ashleigh, Beckie, Beni, Brookie, Debbie, Denise, Elizabeth, Gemma, Gemma, Grace, Hannah, Holly, Jess, Jesse, Jody, Katie, Liz, Lizzie, Lynn, Megan, Michelle, Michelle, Monique, Natalie, Natalie, Rebecca, Thabani, Vicky, and Victoria.

The carers were supported by Philip (Bluebird Care), John (Right at Home), Liz (AMG Healthcare) and their office teams in keeping all the schedules on track and maintaining the very highest quality of care throughout, which was reflected in their respective CQC inspections.

Towards the end of Sue's time we had care 24 hours a day, seven days a week, normally consisting of one carer in the house and often two carers.

Sometimes it was difficult to keep track of who was coming and going. Some carers were with us less than a month, as Sue put each of the new carers through their paces. She could be very demanding, and her needs got complicated as time wore on. Some of the carers were new to the care business and disappeared quickly, whilst others stayed the distance and had their "carer cherry popped" to quote one of them. At the other end of the spectrum we had some carers who stayed with us for nearly the whole of the journey.

My focus was to ensure that the carers could do their job in the best way possible in order for Sue to receive the best attention. I never needed to have worried though as the team were always amazing. They all cared and did their best to ensure Sue was looked after. Having a great care team gave me constant reassurance, as I knew someone would be in the house to look after Sue whilst I was at work.

...to the dedicated healthcare professionals...

In addition to the carers there were over 250 healthcare professionals across the 50 specialist and healthcare teams involved in Sue's diagnosis and treatment. Every one of you showed empathy, compassion and support. You helped us to overcome everything that MSA threw at us.

Unfortunately, I cannot name everyone, but I just want to say thank you to all of you for your guidance, support and care throughout our journey.

Supporting us throughout and afterwards were the best team of GPs, Practice Nurses and Community Nurses based at Appletree Medical Practice in Duffield. You supported Sue from the moment she was born, throughout all her illnesses and in her final hours. You also supported and encouraged me throughout the journey. It is a privilege to have such a caring team looking after us all in Duffield.

The ever-present Dr Bajaj was our lead consultant. You ensured that we sailed the best course possible, made sure we understood what was happening and what might happen, and gave us constant encouragement that we were doing well. You were always at the end of the phone or email and had an amazing bed-side manner when we saw you. As a result, we never felt alone.

...to the UK MSA Trust...

You helped us as we struggled to come to terms with the MSA diagnosis, answered our questions so we understood what MSA was and the challenges ahead, and gave us support when we needed it.

I am truly inspired by your relentless focus on finding a way to prevent or treat this cruel illness, raising awareness and supporting fellow people with MSA.

...everyone else who helped us...

I have lost count of everyone who helped us on our journey. Many of you appear through the stories I have told in this book, but we have so many other stories and memories. A big thank you to all of you.

...and to my beautiful wife, partner, and best friend: Tiger

Thank you for letting me be a part of your life. You enriched every aspect of my life and made me the man I am today. I miss you every minute of the day and just wish we had had more time together.

Part II

Some hints and tips

I would like to share some hints and tips from our journey which will hopefully help and may be of use to others starting down, or already on, the MSA journey or other chronic or terminal illnesses.

These do not replace the need to seek and follow advice from medical or other professionals. Of course, only use medication prescribed by a professional.

Searching for a diagnosis and better understanding

Do not give up searching until you have the answer you feel happy with. We kept looking even after the diagnosis of early onset Parkinson's disease as it did not explain everything.

Do not be afraid to ask for a second opinion. Every consultant has different knowledge and experiences so a second opinion may also provide different insights.

There is no such thing as a "stupid question". It does not matter how trivial it may seem at the time; you never know what you might learn.

Ask what is likely to happen and when. With MSA it is difficult to answer this question accurately but there are some things that are more likely to happen than others and by understanding this you will be able to plan. (I have included Sue's timeline as an example).

If an "unexpected" symptom occurs, then review the diagnosis. It is worth understanding the likely and unlikely symptoms of an illness. Question your consultant about why symptoms are happening. It may be that you have a different illness than first diagnosed or that you have a second illness.

Only read information from trusted sources. There is a huge amount of information online but MSA is so rare that the breadth of material is not available currently. I found at the time that the best sources were available from the UK National Health Service and the UK MSA Trust. There is also some good information from USA and Australian MSA charities.

Be cautious of using chat rooms. My experience was that those sharing online chat rooms were highlighting the extreme cases of a symptom rather than the norm. By reading them I was seeing the worst of every symptom.

Getting the most out of appointments

Take someone with you. It can be difficult on your own to remember everything or take it all in especially when you are asking the questions and receiving information about a diagnosis or test result.

Write down all your symptoms and changes. It helps to write down new symptoms or changes to existing symptoms in order not to forget anything. Capturing anything that makes the symptoms worse or if they get worse at different times of the day will help the healthcare professional decide a course of action.

Writing down all your medication in advance will save precious time as most healthcare professionals will ask and review medications. This will leave more time for your questions

Write down all your questions and worries and leave some space for the answers. This will ensure you ask all your questions. It will also give the consultant the chance to address your worries and make suggestions that can help.

Arrive early so you can review your questions before walking into the appointment.

Write down their answers. This allows you time to process the information so you can ask follow-up questions. Reading out the answer enables you to confirm what the healthcare professional has said and to check the spelling of words and review the answers after the appointment.

Clarify their answers. If you do not understand something, ask them to explain.

Do not be rushed during the appointment, especially if the consultant is running late. You need to make sure all your concerns and questions are addressed and that you fully understand everything that the consultant might say. Make sure you understand the significance of any scans and test results, and the next steps.

Ask how to contact the professional. We all think of questions we wished we had asked after an appointment.

Ask for a copy of all the correspondence and test results. You have the right to know what healthcare professionals are writing about you and this will ensure you have a better understanding of the diagnosis and treatments. It also allows you to check that what is being said accurately reflects the current situation and what was discussed.

As an example, we once had a letter sent to our GP where the notes were mixed-up. It was somewhat understandable as, coincidentally, another patient with the same name had been in the clinic at the same time.

Carve out some time afterwards to talk about the appointment. We always reviewed appointments together to discuss how it had gone and what we wanted to do differently either for Sue's care or the next time we spoke to the professional.

Partnering with the medical professionals

View the medical professionals as partners. They are there to help you treat or cope with an illness and have the same aim. Speak with them in an open and honest way.

Develop a strong relationship. You need to be able to reach out at any time so put the effort in to developing a relationship.

The importance of the relationship between medical professional and patient is now widely recognised under the concept of **"Patients as Partners (PP)"**. This is especially the case with MSA as it is not just the healthcare professionals providing the care.

Check understanding of MSA. It is such a rare and complex illness that many healthcare professionals may not have come across a person with MSA before and each person's journey is unique. It is worth exploring their experience and taking the time to explain what MSA is and how it is affecting the person with MSA.

Increase your own awareness. The more you understand about the illness the better the conversation you can have and the better the decision.

Take control of the conversations and timelines. If you are unhappy with the intervals between appointments, then raise the issue and ask for more regular meetings especially as the illness progresses.

Discuss and jointly own the decisions. In my experience any decision should be based on the medical / scientific knowledge of the healthcare professional AND the individual experiences that you are having of the illness.

It is **important that healthcare professionals understand your concerns, objectives and goals** so they have your "best interests" at heart. Take the time to explain what you want and why.

Do not be afraid to ask for a Multi-Disciplinary Team (MDT) review. This brings all the relevant healthcare professionals together in a face-to-face meeting and ensures that everyone is aware of the current status.

Coming to terms personally with a diagnosis

Give yourself permission to deal with a diagnosis in any way you see fit and do not be critical of your emotions. Create the space and time you need to come to terms with it.

Talk, but only when and if you feel ready. Talking about the diagnosis and your feelings can help to process the situation. Not everyone knows how to start the conversation or what to say so do not be upset if people stop reaching out or if they ask questions in what seems to be an inconsiderate way. If you want to talk to someone independent, then consider a counsellor who can help you with advice and guidance.

If you are not ready to talk or it is too difficult, write down how you feel and what your worries are. This will help shape your thoughts and express them without the emotions overpowering the conversation. It could then be easier for others to read and understand.

Stay close. Maintain the proximity and intimacy of friendships and relationships. Try to keep things as normal as possible without denying what is happening.

Lean on others. Family and friends will likely offer support – do not be afraid to take it nor to ask for help if they have not offered it, as they may simply not know what to say.

Try to continue to do things that you enjoy right until the end. The journey does not need to be a totally negative experience no matter how hard or difficult it might be. Focus energy and effort into arranging the things that will make the journey easier, rather than worrying about the inevitable outcome.

"Bucket List". Is there anything you particularly want to do? With progressive illnesses like MSA it is important to do these earlier rather than later, even though the early stages of MSA are often taken up by getting a diagnosis. You will be surprised by what you can still do with a bit of careful planning and help.

Don't worry when the illness progresses quickly as it can progress more slowly at other times. We found that the illness progressed at different rates, for example, the rate of decline was rapid in 2017 and 2018 but slowed in 2019 with smaller deteriorations.

Supporting someone affected by the diagnosis

Treat the person normally. Minimise changes to the way that you interact or the conversations you have. It is important that the illness does not dominate the relationship or conversation any more than it needs to.

Continue to involve the person in decisions and asking them if they would like to get involved in activities, trips or events. Don't make assumptions about what they would like to do or whether they would be able to do something.

Listen. Show empathy and support. Listen to what they are saying and try not to criticise or change the subject.

Chose and ask your questions about the illness carefully so you don't cause additional anxiety or worry. For example, avoid asking questions about what may or may not happen in the future.

Offer to be there for them whenever they need you. Offer to do something specific rather than a generic offer of help.

Getting ready for the journey and planning ahead

Visit the UK MSA Trust website and talk to MSA Nursing team. There is excellent advice on what to expect and you can talk through the typical journey and think about adaptations and equipment that will help.

Create a support network comprising of family, friends, and work colleagues. Set clear boundaries and ways that they can help you. Use online communities and support groups if/when they help you.

Keep a diary or planner so everyone is clear what appointments and other key events are happening, when and where. I put travel time in the diary, so we always arrived on time.

Establish a clear routine but maintain flexibility to ensure that everyone knows what should be done and when and to check that the tasks had been done.

Consider Advance Care Planning. This is a discussion with healthcare professionals to understand future wishes and priorities for care. It will likely cover the illness and/or prognosis; options available for treatment; wishes, preferences, priorities and concerns; and any specific treatments that should not be undertaken. It is also worth identifying someone to speak on behalf of the person with the illness if they are not able to do so themselves and appointing someone to make healthcare decisions using a lasting power of attorney.

The discussion can be held at any stage of the illness and the outcome is an **Advanced Care Plan** which can be shared with healthcare professionals should decisions need to be made when the person who is ill is unable to communicate or lacks capacity.

A ReSPECT (Recommended Summary Plan for Emergency Care and Treatment) form focuses on what should be done in an emergency and helps family and healthcare providers take the most appropriate action including prioritising life sustainment vs. comfort, specific types of care that should / should not be given, and whether CPR should be performed.

Check any life / critical illness insurance. These can help pay for costs you may incur. It is worth ensuring that the details of any life insurance reflect your current wishes.

Check your will to ensure that your wishes are followed, especially as the rules for inheritance in the absence of a will are not straight forward and life changes can mean wills become out of date quickly.

Put in place lasting power of attorney (health & wealth) so the right person can make decisions on both health and wealth as the person with MSA becomes incapacitated. The attorney (person acting on your behalf) must act in your best interests.

Have the right conversations early so you can discuss each other's concerns and goals. These conversations are so much harder when communication becomes more difficult.

Talk to an occupational therapist to advise you on changes to make in the house to make things easier and safer. This should be a regular dialogue as the illness progresses.

Perform a Health and Safety check of the house because changes to mobility increase the risks of trips and falls. For example, look for things such as loose rugs and untidy cables, and make them safe. Light up areas that are dim if possible.

Make the house adaptations early. I cannot stress enough the benefits of making adaptations to the house before you need them. It removes the stress of waiting for builders and suppliers to deliver the equipment and/or make the changes at a time when you urgently need them. These adaptations reduce the risk of the person injuring themselves and could include:

- Ramps to enter and leave the house
- Handrails to help moving around the house
- Stairlifts to go up and down the stairs safely
- Raised toilet seats to assist getting on and off the toilet
- Downstairs bathroom including shower area

There is funding available to help with some of the above adaptations.

Get the equipment in before you need it. I have included a list of the equipment we found helpful through this and the "Managing Symptoms" chapters. There is plenty of equipment that will make everyone's lives easier, more comfortable, and ensure you can carry on doing things for as long as possible.

Consider writing letters or recording a video. Sue wrote three letters, which let me know how she felt and what she wanted me to do after she passed away. They were upsetting and reassuring in equal measure. It is worth acknowledging that these do reflect feelings and wishes at a particular moment in time and might be different if they were written at another point on the journey.

Look for ways to make the journey easier. There are so many things you can do to make your journey easier. I found that the simplest things helped reduce the workload, for example, having medication delivered and help from the council regarding having more waste bins and help moving the bins on collection day.

To avoid urgent trips to pharmacies, **ask about an "anticipatory medication" pack**. Your GP or Palliative Services will recommend what it could include, so for example, strong pain-killers and anti-sickness drugs will be in place and ready to be used by on-call doctors and nurses as necessary.

Places to go to get help

Create, use and refresh your support network of family, friends and work colleagues. Throughout our journey we used each person in our support network in different ways as we all have strengths that help in a particular circumstance. With progressive illnesses like MSA that stretch over many years the people in your support network will naturally change, as will your needs.

Talk to your GP. You need to be proactive and drive the conversations. In theory you will have a nominated GP and it is worth sharing information on MSA with them. There may also be a clinical practitioner that specialises in patients with complex clinical cases. In our case it was Heidi who was superb throughout.

Make your GP's Care Coordinator your "best friend". The role of the Care Coordinator is to get involved with patients who have the most complex care needs and bring together the different specialists to ensure the right care is being provided and to monitor and evaluate it. We were lucky to have an amazing Care Coordinator called June.

Patient Participation Groups (PPG) and/or Patient Advice and Liaison Services (PALS). These groups exist to act as an interface between patients and medical organisations, to provide advice on generic issues such as "where to go for…" and can put you in touch with support groups operating in the community or acute care settings.

Social Services will be able to allocate a social worker who can help with the day to day challenges caused by MSA. Social care is means tested but they can put you in touch with a wide variety of organisations and, ultimately, funding.

UK National Health Service (NHS) will provide a significant amount of the care and can also provide funding for care being provided in the community.

Other organisations such as charities and religious groups can provide equipment, advice, guidance and support including respite care for carers to provide them with the opportunity to recharge their batteries.

Counselling and bereavement services are available to talk through your worries and concerns.

Government organisations such as local council and HMRC can provide advice and guidance on benefits available and tax reliefs.

Notify your electricity supplier that you have someone dependent on continuous electricity supply. They will have priority services including a phone number to call in the event of a power issue.

Remap is a UK charity that custom-makes equipment to help disabled people and those with severe illnesses live more independently.

Places to go to get information

The main sources of information used on our journey were:

Medical and **Healthcare professionals.**

Reputable medical websites (e.g. UK National Health Service).

Charities focused on MSA (e.g. UK MSA Trust), adjacent illnesses (e.g. Parkinson's UK) **or specific symptoms** (e.g. Bladder and Bowel UK).

Support groups are available for people with MSA and carers.

Charities focused on living with disabilities, e.g. Disability Living Foundation.

…and for non-medical information:

Government websites (e.g. for latest funding.)

Local government websites (e.g. for local services)

How to get funding help in the UK

There are many potential sources of funding in the UK to help with the provision of care and support.

Over time these sources, and the policies that apply to them, may change. Rather than list the sources of funding that were available whilst we undertook the journey, I have listed the broad areas to explore.

The task of exploring these options and whether they are applicable is bewildering. I would recommend discussing these with your GP, charities such as the UK MSA trust, and other support groups, as well as looking at reputable internet sites like the UK government.

Government funding:

1. Payments for **care provision** in the domestic home or care home setting. This may cover some, if not all, of the extra costs associated with having a long-term illness or disability.

   It is worth noting that there may be different levels of payment dependent on criteria covering the impact of the illness on every-day tasks such as preparing food, eating and drinking, washing and bathing, toileting needs, dressing and undressing, communicating, reading, mixing with other people, making decisions about money, going out, moving around, and anything else that might be relevant; complexity of medication and treatment; and, the prognosis. It is therefore important to discuss the full impact on the person with the illness.

You can find out more about our experience of applying for care funding in the chapter called “Afternoon tea at the Ritz”.

2. Payments for **specialised care** may also be available if the care needs to be provided by, for example, a registered nurse, rather than a personal assistant / social carer.

3. Benefits which may help with the **cost of prescriptions and drugs**.

4. **Mobility-related** benefits that may help with the increased costs of remaining mobile, e.g. in purchasing or leasing a wheelchair accessible vehicle.

5. **Work-related** benefits that may help to offset any impact to earning potential, for example, if the person with MSA has to give up work.

6. **Age-related** benefits may be applicable if, for example, the person with MSA has retired. There may be additional allowances and/or changes to pension payments.

7. **Carer-related** benefits may be applicable for the person who is providing care to a partner or family member.

8. **Provision of equipment** on a temporary or permanent basis. For example, four-way profiling bed, standing aids, and hoists. Occupational therapists should be able to advise on what is needed and where it can be sourced from, for example, the UK National Health Service.

9. **Government grants** to help with costs, e.g. to cover house adaptations.

10. **Reductions in taxation**. For example, local council tax as a result of adaptations and/or occupancy rates.

11. **Tax exemptions** may exist, for example, when adapting buildings for disabled use, the purchase of goods intended specifically for people with disabilities, or vehicle road tax.

12. Continually check **existing benefits** as there may be changes to the benefit available as a result of MSA being diagnosed or the illness progressing.

13. **Other allowances** may be applicable, for example, to help with bereavement and funeral costs.

Other sources of funding:

14. Some **charities** provide grants to cover costs. They can also potentially provide equipment, avoiding the cost of purchasing or renting it, or provide free alterations or repairs.

15. **Hospices** may be able to provide free temporary or respite care. Some hospices also offer free services such as counselling, activities and complementary therapies.

16. Help with **utility and other household bills**, e.g. funding, reducing or phasing payments

17. **Critical Care and Life Insurances** may pay out on diagnosis of a critical or terminal illness.

18. **Blue Badge** may allow free car parking but note that not all disabled spaces are free.

19. **Other benefits** may be applicable, for example, to help with bereavement and funeral costs.

Other considerations regarding funding:

20. **Discuss with your GP or other support organisations** to see if there is anything they can do to help facilitate funding discussions. For example, our GP completed a DS1500 form. This is a factual statement by a GP about a person's condition, the clinical features that indicate rate of progression, and treatment. It is more commonly mentioned for people with cancer and ensures they get the right level of care in the case of a terminal illness, i.e. where life expectancy is expected to be below six months. Due to the nature of MSA no one knows the duration of the journey, so it is a judgement call when this is appropriate. Whilst it does not guarantee funding will be granted it can result in the higher rate of benefits being approved and is not means tested.

Selecting and working with care companies

Decide what care you are looking for:

- where care will be provided (domiciliary)
- types of carer (care worker vs. personal assistant)
- presence (visits vs. full time vs. live-in)
- duration (regular hours, all day and/or night)
- what needs doing (daily activities and/or personal care)
- complexity (medication, PEG feeding, etc.)
- contracting (direct vs. agency).

Identify possible care companies. There are several different sources to find care companies including family and friends, NHS and Council websites, UK Homecare Association (UKHCA), and Care Quality Commission (CQC). You can also ask the GP Care Coordinator for their recommendations.

Create a shortlist of care companies. Ask friends and family to see if they know anyone. On the internet you can find the reviews by the Care Quality Commission and other reviews, e.g. on the NHS website.

Meet and interview the shortlisted care companies. Prepare a list of questions and write down their answers so you can compare later. Suggested questions include:

- what experience do they have of MSA or other complex, demanding and progressive illnesses?

- how do they recruit and what checks are done?

- what turnover of carers do they have?

- how do they train their carers?
- what experience and qualifications do they have?
- will there be a consistent team involved? Will they be all male, female or mixed?
- what reviews do they do of the care being provided?
- how easily and quickly can they respond to evolving and increasing needs?
- how will they handle illness and holidays?
- what are the charges for days, weekends and nights?
- what happens in an emergency?
- are they able to provide care funded by the NHS?
- what are the standard terms and conditions?

Be aware of minimum call times. Check that the company can offer you the visit duration you need. However, be cautious of care companies that are happy to do 15-minute visits. In such a short window it is very difficult to do the tasks required and provide the personal touch.

Being comfortable. The questions above will examine how the company will provide care, but it is equally important that you can work together and trust them. If you feel uncomfortable in the visit it is worth exploring why.

Check what other people think. It is worth asking for references and seeing what their other customers think about both care coordination and care provision.

Build a rapport with the care coordination team. Most care companies have a back-office team that coordinates the care and deals with issues when they arise. It helps if they know you personally and that you are easy to deal with. I always asked some of the team to visit us, so they knew Sue as a real person rather than a name on a spreadsheet. It also helped if they understood the environment their carers were working in.

Agree who is in charge. Clearly you are ultimately in charge, but it is useful to have a lead carer who is keeping an eye on everything and a lead care company if multiple care companies are involved.

Agree the care plan. This is an important document that should describe the illness, care needs, the care to be provided, likes and dislikes, etc. Have a thorough discussion on the care plan and review it regularly.

Insist on getting a rota in advance. It is important that you know who is coming and when. This demonstrates their planning and allows you to check on their reliability.

Request that all new carers to the team shadow existing carers. MSA is a complex illness and each person with MSA has unique needs. To ensure that the right quality of care is provided new carers, especially those new to the care industry, should spend time watching how the care is currently provided and what does / does not work. You should not be charged for the shadowing.

Make the carers feel welcome. It is amazing that people have different attitudes towards carers. My view is that if the carers feel welcome in your home then that kindness is passed on to the person they are caring for. Allow them to make themselves tea and coffee and use the toilet. Be polite and friendly and have a bit of a laugh with them.

Read the daily logs. This provides insight into the care being provided, any problems or issues, general observations, etc.

Not all carers are suitable. It's worth doing a few spot checks and privately discuss any observations to reassure yourself of the quality of care being provided. Be prepared to say no to a specific carer, even if it is simply a personality clash.

Safe moving and handling

Ask to be trained in moving and handling. Moving or lifting someone without proper training puts everyone involved at risk of injury. Whilst carers and medical professionals are trained in the safe moving and handling of patients it is not routinely provided to relatives. Carers, medical professionals and equipment suppliers can demonstrate how to do moving and handling safely.

Dealing with emergencies

Create an emergency contacts and information folder in case something goes wrong. Having information readily to hand helps to takes the pressure off. My recommendation is that you create a dedicated folder that contains the following (and in a suggested order):

- Reminder to call 111 or 999 for emergencies.

- Contact names & details for non-emergencies (this could include neighbours if they agree).

- The personal details of the person with MSA:
  - full name
  - address including postcode
  - date of birth
  - medical conditions
  - medication
  - any allergies
  - summary of express wishes, e.g. ReSPECT form
  - lasting power of attorney (if given).

- List of contacts and their details (this should include full names, relationship, landline and mobile, email, addresses, alternative contact name plus any notes of caution, e.g. what should / should not be said to avoid upsetting the contacts).

- List of professional contacts and their details (this should include main and emergency numbers for each of the care companies, GPs, pharmacist, Community Nursing, consultants, etc.).

- Contact details for any specialist teams that provide out of hours (night-time) support such as RIG feeding team, Palliative Care, etc. plus any specific information if something happens like the RIG tube popping out.

- List of contacts that can help with non-medical issues. This might include electrician, plumber, etc. so issues can be resolved quickly and not impact on care provision.

- Where medication is kept including emergency medical pack and the MARS sheets which record what medication was given, by whom and when.

- Medication routine – summary. List the medication such as drugs, creams, etc., the strength and frequency, plus any optional or "as-required" drugs like Paracetamol. Include a copy of the latest prescription slip. These provide a quick view of the medication.

- Medication routine – timetable. This shows the medication in the order it should be taken and the typical times. That way people, e.g. a paramedic, can quickly understand what medication had been taken by what time and what was left for the rest of the day.

- The ReSPECT form covering what to do in an emergency.

- A copy of the GP's Individual Care Management Plan, which outlines a tailored approach to care, taking into account the wishes of the person with the illness.

Managing symptoms

These are some of the symptoms that we encountered and some of the things we tried. Not everyone will get all these symptoms.

The techniques, advice for carers, equipment, medication and treatments included in this section do not replace the need to seek and follow advice from medical and other professionals.

Note, where medication is listed it has been included as an example to show the type of drug regimes available but only medication prescribed by a professional should be considered.

Communication

Communication including speech, writing and typing can be affected however it is possible to maintain effective and fulfilling communication as the illness progresses:

Techniques:

Patience is critical as it will take longer to convey simple messages and creating a stressful environment or showing frustrations will make it even harder.

Make time for the conversation and don't rush through it.

Remove any distractions such as background music so everyone can focus on the conversation and hear softly spoken words. This also avoids the need to repeat words, which is unnecessarily tiring for the person with MSA.

Stop using superfluous words and only use the minimum set of words for your message to save much needed energy. The Speech & Language Therapist (SALT) said stop using "Please", "Thank you", "Can I have…?", etc and just say, for example, "drink of tea" rather than, "Can I have a drink of tea please?"

Try to get your heads at the same level and maintain eye contact, for example, by kneeling or sitting down next to the wheelchair or raising the bed. Encourage others to do the same. This will make it easier to hear and see each other, plus it is not so intimidating.

Use active listening. This is a technique that can help in all aspects of life but especially when someone is struggling to communicate something more complicated.

There are several elements to active listening such as paying attention, showing you are listening by giving reassuring signs such as smiling and nodding, not interrupting until the person has finished, suspending judgement, asking questions to clarify understanding or the intent and summarising what you have heard.

It also involves watching and interpreting body language.

Keep having conversations and **involve the person with MSA in them** no matter how hard or frustrating it may seem. Encourage others to do the same as they may be reluctant because they do not know how, do not know what to talk about or they are anxious they will make the person tired.

Try to have normal conversations and involve the person with MSA in important decisions. It is okay to still disagree but remember that someone with MSA will not be able to simply get up and walk away if they get upset.

Keep adapting your communication skills. As the illness progresses so will the need to change how you communicate. If you are supporting someone with an illness that affects their ability to communicate, it is worth taking the time to learn and practise new skills and tools. Try using the communication skills and tools yourself – it will give you some empathy on how hard it is for the person with the illness.

Be aware that **MSA can affect the link between how the person is really feeling and how they express it**, for example, laughing at something sad.

Make visitors aware of interests and topics that the person enjoys and ask them to have conversations about those.

Ensure carers have good communication skills. Do not be afraid to ask for a carer to be replaced if they are unable to communicate efficiently and effectively.

Equipment:

Alphabet charts have the alphabet and numbers printed on a single sheet of A4 paper in various layouts that makes spelling words quick and easy. Laminating them is a good idea as these may get used frequently through the day.

It is worth writing down the letters as they are spelt as it can be difficult to remember the start of the sentence by the time you get to the end.

Buzzers are useful to call for help as the person's voice gets quieter and speaking becomes more difficult. There are various types of buzzer that cater for the illness as it progresses but also for the needs of the carers, e.g. emitting noise and/or flashing lights when the buzzer is pressed.

Communication charts are like alphabet charts except they have phrases and are grouped into themes. They allow faster conversations around regular topics such as “I would like a drink of….” or “I need my pad changing”. They can be easily tailored to the needs and interests of the person struggling with communication.

Eye-tracking software and speech. This allows the person to use their eyes to look at an electronic keyboard and list of phrases on a computer screen. Capturing the eye movement, the voice synthesizer then pronounces the words. These devices can also be used to browse the internet, write documents and answer emails.

Joysticks work in the same way as eye-tracking software and allow the person to select words and phrases on a computer.

Voice amplifiers increase the volume of speech as the voice gets quieter.

Voice banks allow the person to capture their voice before it becomes too weak. The recording of their own voice is then used rather than an artificial voice to speak the words captured via computer devices such as the eye-tracking software. This needs to be done early in the illness to be most effective.

Eating and drinking including problems swallowing

People with MSA may initially struggle to prepare food, which can then be followed by challenges in consuming food and drink as a result of posture, movement and swallowing problems.

Techniques:

Ask for an Occupational Therapist to **perform a kitchen assessment.** This will identify ways of making food and drink preparation more manageable. They will perform a health and safety assessment of the kitchen and assess range of movement, balance, motor skills and fitness.

Speech And Language Therapists (SALT) can advise on **how to prepare food and fluids** to make them easier to consume such as making softer food or thickening liquids thereby reducing the risk of coughing or choking.

Watch out for **coughing or throat clearing whilst consuming food or drink,** which may indicate difficulties with swallowing (dysphagia). Speech And Language Therapists can provide strategies and exercises to improve swallowing.

Physiotherapists can provide advice on aspects such as **body and head posture,** which might help swallowing and digestion.

Equipment:

Kitchen equipment that helped food and drink preparation in the early stages of MSA included bottle and jar openers to provide

more grip and leverage, non-slip chopping board, a stool to sit on at the kitchen counter, a kitchen trolley to move things around, kettle tipper and larger handled cooking utensils.

Speech And Language Therapists can advise on how to make **the process of consuming food and fluids less onerous** including use of equipment such as larger-handled cutlery, one-handed cutlery, deep plates, plate guards, insulated plates to keep food hotter for longer, non-slip table mats, two-handled drinking cups, cups with spouts and one-way straws.

Medication and treatments:

A feeding tube called a Percutaneous Endoscopic Gastrostomy (PEG) or a Radiologically Inserted Gastrostomy (RIG) can be fitted. Both allow fluids, food and medication to be given directly into the stomach rather than orally. At the same time, fluids, food and medication can still be taken orally. The difference between a PEG and a RIG is that a PEG is guided using a telescope down the food pipe whilst the RIG is fitted using x-ray guidance.

Emotions

Like any other progressive and terminal illness, the journey with MSA will present many challenges that affect the mood and emotions of the person with MSA, their family, friends and others involved in their care and support.

It is normal to see "negative" emotions such as anger, anxiety, confusion, denial, envy, fear, frustration, helplessness, resentment, and sadness. The strength of these emotions can overwhelm, leading to physical symptoms, relationship issues, social isolation and questioning the meaning of everything.

There will be times when the "positive" emotions dominate the mood including acceptance, amusement, courage, excitement, forgiveness, gratitude, happiness, love, peace, pride and relief.

There will even be times when there is no emotion with the focus being purely on the task at hand.

Our journey was an emotional roller coaster where we experienced all of these and more. At times we were aligned and sharing the same highs and lows. At other times we experienced different emotions sometimes hiding them to "protect" each other. Looking back, I believe that we had more time experiencing the positive emotions than the negative ones.

Techniques:

Accept that it is okay and perfectly normal to have good and bad moments.

Keep doing things that improve intimacy such as holding hands, hugging, kissing, listening to music, reading together, reminiscing, sharing a joke and going out.

Maintain **positive mindset** and focus on **making the journey as good as possible** for everyone involved.

Sleep, rest and slowing down are needed to allow the body and mind to recover.

Just smiling will create a more positive mood or response.

Talking and reflecting about what is happening, your worries and concerns is one of the most powerful ways to boost your mood.

Time management and breaking tasks into manageable chunks will help prevent becoming overwhelmed by the magnitude of everything that is happening and what needs to be done.

Medication and treatments:

In the early stages of the illness Sue enjoyed **Pilates** and I think that this helped maintain her strength and coordination for as long as possible. Pilates is a form of **"active therapy"**. These involve the person exerting effort to stimulate and relax muscles, reduce stress and/or improve their mood. Other examples of active therapies include art, music and tai chi.

Cognitive behavioural therapy, guided self-help and counselling can all help by talking with a trained therapist.

Medication such as antidepressants and relaxants can also help.

The things that really helped Sue's mood as the illness progressed were **manicures, massages, music, reflexology and the smell from scented candles.** These are known as **"passive therapies"** that involve using equipment or activities to stimulate or relax muscles, reduce stress or improve the mood without having to exert any effort.

Distraction also helped Sue's mood and she enjoyed planning events and outings, talking and listening to visitors, having her hair styled, dressing up to go out, organising lists of things for me to do, and telling me that I had not done things to an acceptable standard.

Eyes

MSA may affect vision in several ways such as blurred or double vision, clarity of vision and field of vision. Eyelids can be affected with insufficient blinking, rapid blinking or struggling to open the eyelids. They can also become itchy, sore, red or swollen.

Techniques:

Have **regular, more frequent eye tests** by an optician to monitor eye health.

Monitor eye and eyelid health, for example, to spot styes and inflammation. Keep checking the person with MSA for jerky or slow eye movement as this can cause blurred or double vision. Note that low blood pressure can also result in vision issues so should be considered when trying to address the problem.

Kneel by the person with MSA to maintain eye contact and minimise the impact on field of vision caused by changes in head posture, for example, where the head tilts forward and down.

Equipment:

Switch to glasses if you wear contact lenses. Have **different glasses for long and short distance** as bi-focals require movement of the eyes and head, which can become more difficult. Consider **magnifying glasses & lenses** to improve small print or **glasses that are larger or have prisms** to provide a wider visual field.

Dark sunglasses can improve the clarity of vision and reduce eye discomfort, if it is affected by bright lights (glare).

Use of **reclining seats / wheelchairs** and the **raising and reclining of beds** can also help improve the field of vision if it is being affected by head posture.

Medicine and treatments:

Consider **eye drops or sprays** where eyes become dry, sore or tired.

Warm compresses or **eye baths** can help to soothe and cleanse eyelids. Try to avoid cross contamination.

Injections into the eyelids can help where someone has a problem opening their eyes.

Hands and arms

MSA can affect the hands, arms and fingers including involuntary movement, rigidity or stiffness (dystonia), cramping, clenching, slow movement (bradykinesia), weakness and a lack of coordination. It can also affect the body's ability to regulate temperature resulting in hot or cold hands.

Techniques:

Massages and other forms of physiotherapy can help relax the muscles and are also good for the emotional state.

If finger clenching occurs, then remember to regularly manicure **fingernails** as they can be painful when pressed into the palm of the hand. This also maintains nail health.

Equipment:

Equipment to help with specific tasks can be recommended by an Occupational Therapist following an assessment of the ability to perform specific tasks, for example, bathing, dressing, drinking, eating, household chores, moving and handling, personal and toiletries. As the MSA is progressive it is worth repeating the assessments on a regular basis. In terms of specific equipment, there are simply too many to list however there are some very good charity websites that can provide an insight. When buying equipment bear in mind that MSA is progressive so it is likely to have a short shelf life.

Gloves, hot water bottles, microwaveable heating pads, air fans, cooling fans, cold pads and cooling towels are very effective at managing the rapid and uncontrolled temperature variations that can occur. The use of bed sheets and blankets versus a duvet allows layers to be added and removed as required to get the right temperature.

Splints are effective in stabilising and supporting the wrist. They relieve pressure, ease discomfort and can delay contractures (shortening of muscles) occurring. Splints should be shaped to match exactly the angle of the person's wrist, hand and fingers so I would recommend only using those tailored by professional physiotherapists (vs. ones available on commercial websites).

Towels and cushions are a simple, cost effective way to support the arms, wrists and hands. In addition, we found **small, soft cuddly toys**, (e.g. the rat) were perfect to hold in the hand and stop fingernails being clenched into the palm of the hand.

Medication and treatments:

Injections into rigid or stiff muscles can relax them. These need to be repeated every three months and the strength of the injection may need to be increased over time to avoid causing muscle weakness.

Drugs that **increase levels of dopamine** may be prescribed as the lack of dopamine affects movement and rigidity.

Relaxants can also help. Changes to dosage levels and the timing of drug administration can improve rigidity.

Infections

The risk of infections, for example, urinary tract and chest infections, is high. It is especially important to be aware of this risk as the usual signs of such infections may not be apparent in a person with MSA because of the effect MSA has on the autonomic nervous system.

Techniques:

It might seem obvious but ensure that everyone **washes their hands** as contact transmission is one of the two main ways that infections can be spread.

Ensure that carers wear **disposable aprons, gloves and other personal protection equipment (PPE)** when performing any care tasks that carry a higher risk of contamination such as personal care and PEG feeding. Aprons, gloves and PPE should be changed between different tasks and after completing tasks.

Ask visitors and carers to stay away if they have a cold and insist that care companies send a replacement carer if the scheduled one is not able to attend due to being ill. Airborne / respiratory transmission is the second major way that infection is spread, and colds and flu pose a significant risk to people with MSA.

Ensure the **safe management and disposal of waste (e.g. used pads) and body fluids.** Keep an eye on how people handle this as it's very easy to let standards drop when under pressure, e.g. if the person with MSA is suffering from diarrhoea.

Keep the environment clean especially where food and medications are prepared.

Keep food and medication in the right environment. For example, once opened, enteral tube feed normally needs to be stored in the fridge and disposed of within 24 hours.

Equipment should be cleaned and maintained regularly. This is especially the case for things like CPAP face-masks, suction yankauers (solid plastic tubes) and equipment used for personal care.

Keep clothes and bedding clean especially after episodes of incontinence.

Review the **standard infection control precautions** that the care company is proposing to implement and ensure they are included in the care plan. Guidance can be found on the NHS website under "Community Infection Prevention and Control Policy for Domiciliary Care Staff".

Watch out for rapid changes in physical or mental state. Some changes can be quite subtle, others more obvious, but it is often the speed of change from one day to the next that is critical to spot, for example, in levels of alertness, breathing patterns or sound.

Always seek medical help if you suspect there may be an infection. A medical practitioner will not criticise you for checking with them to see if everything is ok, no matter how often you do this.

Equipment:

A baby steriliser can be used to disinfect items such as the syringes used in PEG feeding.

Urinary dipsticks, thermometer, blood pressure and oxygen saturation monitors can be kept in case they are needed in the house. However, these should not be an alternative to seeking timely professional medical advice.

Medication & treatments:

Ensure you adhere to medical advice on things that help with infections such as vaccinations and completing courses of medication, especially antibiotics and steroid creams to avoid the infection returning and being more resistant.

Legs and feet

The MSA challenges with legs, feet and toes are very similar to those that occur with arms, hands and fingers. As a result, most of the techniques, advice for carers, equipment and medication are similar. This section covers the equipment and medication or treatment that is unique to legs, feet, and toes.

Equipment:

Orthotic ankle boots and heel protectors can help support the ankle in the same manner as splints for wrists. However, we found rolled up towels and cushions also helped support Sue's feet in bed and were washable and easy to reposition.

Massage and circulation machines can help relieve aches and pains and reduce swelling. Foot spas can also help to relieve aches and pains.

Medication and treatments:

Raise feet to reduce swelling (oedema) but check blood pressure.

Medication can help to **decrease fluid congestion.**

Mouth and oral care

MSA does not cause specific issues with the mouth however many of the MSA symptoms affect the ability of a person with the illness to maintain good mouth and oral hygiene. For example, too little saliva can cause gums, tongue and other tissues to become swollen and uncomfortable whilst it can also accelerate tooth decay.

Techniques:

Regularly check mouth health. Communication and movement issues may hamper the person with MSA from saying what the problem is and where.

Increase visits to the dentist for regular reviews of oral health and to ensure early intervention if required.

You may need to be referred to a dentist who can treat people with specialist needs. This service is typically provided by the NHS Community Dental Services who are in more accessible buildings (hospitals, specialist health centres, mobile clinics or home visits), have more space for wheelchairs and are more experienced than a regular dentist in dealing with people who have, for example, posture issues.

Medication and treatments:

Use high fluoride, non-foaming toothpaste to maintain teeth health and minimise risk of choking.

Movement: posture, bearing, balance, and strength

MSA can affect a person's ability to move in four ways:

1. posture – the position of the person's body
2. bearing – the way the person stands or moves
3. balance – the way the person remains steady and upright
4. strength – the effort required by the person to move.

The effects on these four areas may result in the person with MSA needing help when moving. Doing this in the wrong way presents a risk to their health as well as injuries to the people providing assistance. Getting advice on a regular basis and doing it the right way is critical.

Techniques:

Request **formal training** on safe moving and handling techniques and how to operate any equipment.

Try out new equipment yourself so you know how it works and feels, for example, get someone else to put you in a hoist and be lifted. It will give you **great insight about how the person with MSA will feel**. For example, they may feel humiliated, vulnerable or unsafe.

When you are doing something new it is worth **pausing, thinking through** what you are going to do, and **then doing it.**

Always **check the safety of what you are about to do,** especially as you become increasingly confident, as this is when mistakes are more likely to happen.

Do not physically lift the person with MSA on your own without using equipment. This puts their health at risk and will put massive strain on your back. Maintaining your own health is important throughout the MSA journey

Perform regular assessments of the person's ability to move and the most appropriate ways to provide assistance

Constantly review the effort and safety of a single person providing moving and handling and consider the need to switch to two people performing the tasks.

Equipment:

There are a **variety of hoists** such as ceiling or mobile hoists to safely and easily lift and move a person. There are also a **wide variety of slings** such as disposable, comfort, toileting and waterproof. An occupational therapist can advise on the most appropriate.

A portable **handy bar** (for the car) can help get in and out of a car. This fits into the car door bracket and provides a temporary supporting handle.

A **riser recliner seat** helps standing up and sitting down. It also ensures a more comfortable sitting experience as a result of the ability to adjust the seat. It can reduce the risk of pressure sores by changing the sitting position and can help with circulation by raising and supporting legs and feet.

Slide sheets reduce the effort of moving and repositioning a person by reducing the friction between the person and the surface they are lying on. It works by rolling the person on to their side, inserting the slide sheet, moving the person on to their other side to complete the positioning of the slide sheet and then using the slide sheet to move the person in any direction. Be very careful about leaving slide sheets on the floor as they are exceptionally slippery.

An alternative to the temporary slide sheets mentioned above is a **slide sheet that is similar to normal bedding**. There are two parts to this: a base sheet which fits around the mattress and has a combination of slippery and grip fabric, and a second sheet that is slippery on one side and soft on the other side (which the person with MSA sleeps on and feels like a normal sheet). This combination then allows the carers to perform movement tasks without having to roll the person with MSA onto their side and insert the slide sheet. There are various makes on the market.

Stairlifts provide a safe alternative to walking up and down stairs and can be fitted to any shape and size of staircase. If possible, it is worth looking for one that can also be operated by the carer.

Simple **standing aid frames** provide manual assistance to the person as they stand up and sit down in a chair.

Mobile stand aids with harnesses are used to help someone as they stand up, sit down and transfer between a chair, wheelchair and bed. They are intended for use whilst the person can still load-bear. To use it the person wears a harness to keep them safe and secure. They put their feet onto a foot plate that allows the standing aid to move whilst the person is supported.

A **"Tilt in Space" chair** provides full flexibility in adjusting the seating position, i.e. the person can adjust the angle of the backrest, seat, leg and foot supports. A big advantage is that having got the right angle between the backrest and the seat, the whole chair can then be tilted backwards whilst maintaining the angle between the backrest, seat, leg and footrests. Most tilt in space chairs also have riser features to help the person get in and out of the chair, and a fully reclined mode that allows the person to lie down.

There are many benefits of a "tilt in space" chair that you may wish to discuss with healthcare professionals including:

- supporting posture and eye contact
- increasing and maintaining comfort
- assisting with repositioning in the chair
- helping with saliva control
- maintaining blood pressure
- alleviating pressure points and risk of pressure sores
- reducing leg swelling
- stability in the chair and reducing the risk of falling out.

Turning cushions can help the process of repositioning where the person needs to sit down and then turn, for example, when sitting in a car seat.

Transfer turntables can help to turn a person smoothly and easily when they are standing, for example, when moving from a bed to a wheelchair. The person needs to be able to weight-bear and maintain their balance.

Walking sticks help to maintain balance when walking. A walking stick with three or four feet provides a more stable aid.

Walking frames can provide additional help with balance and mobility. An alternative is a **wheeled walking frames** or **rollator.** However, there is a risk that these might cause slips or falls in people with balance issues, as the wheels can run away from the person as they lean on them. A physiotherapist can advise on the most appropriate aid.

There are many types of **manual and electric wheelchairs** that can be used to maintain mobility and allow the person with MSA to be comfortable in a seated position for long periods of time. Wheelchair Services can provide advice on the right wheelchair. They will assess:

- what the chair will be used for
- getting in and out of the chair
- whether an attendant is needed to move the chair
- how long you will be sitting in the chair
- posture and ability to remain stable while sitting
- weight and height to get the right size of wheelchair
- risk of pressure sores.

Wheelchair Accessible Vehicles (WAVs) allow the person with MSA to go out on longer trips whilst remaining seated in the wheelchair. Things we considered when selecting were:

- size of the wheelchair (e.g. tilt-in-space are larger)
- automated vs. manual ramps and doors
- front or rear location for the wheelchair user
- how many other people will need to be in the WAV
- view for the wheelchair user out of the windscreen
- size of the WAV.

Saliva

Saliva maintains oral health and facilitates swallowing and speech. Effective management of saliva production is critical as saliva issues can lead to problems with eating, talking, oral infections and chapped lips alongside anxiety and low self-esteem. As swallowing reflexes worsen, the risk of choking and chest infections can increase. There are typically three types of problem: too much, too thick and too little saliva.

Techniques:

Increasing fluids can help to thin saliva.

Balm tissues seem better for wiping away excess saliva and are more hygienic and kinder. They can be used to protect clothing and are less conspicuous than soggy handkerchiefs or flannels.

Vaseline can help to protect the lips from chaffing.

Equipment:

Oral swabs were very helpful when we had to remove too much or too thick saliva, especially when travelling. Oral swabs dipped in fruit teas can be used to cleanse and freshen the mouth (avoid acidic fluids that can damage tooth enamel). Caution is needed to avoid choking on the swab.

Posture changes including reclining in a wheelchair or chair can help the saliva drain to the back of the mouth.

Steam nebulisers can help with saliva production and thickness.

A suction machine is very effective for removing large quantities or very thick saliva. Our suction machine had battery power so we could still use it on our trips and outings.

Medication and treatments:

Artificial saliva available in gel and spray form can freshen the mouth and help with chewing and swallowing.

Regular **injections** every three to four months into the saliva glands proved to be very effective at stopping or reducing the production of saliva, usually within ten days of the injection.

Changes to **food and drinks** can have a natural effect in drying the mouth, thinning saliva or making swallowing easier. Avoid items that pose a choke risk.

Medication can be used to **dry out the mouth** whilst there are drugs that can be used to **thin out saliva**.

Swallowing exercises can help remove excess saliva and reduce pooling of saliva at the front of the mouth and on the chin.

Toothbrushes can also be used in the same way as oral swabs to remove excess or thick saliva.

Skin and hair care

MSA and the way that care is provided can affect skin condition. Common problems include tearing or bruising, pressure sores, moisture lesions, dryness and other sores, fragility, and cuts and scrapes. These can be caused by loss of mobility, poor handling techniques, inadequate washing and drying, and poor hydration and nutrition. Also consider that the risk of pressure sores increases as levels of mobility decrease.

Techniques:

Perform **regular risk assessments** to identify potential skin integrity issues. The two methods most commonly used are:

- Waterlow Pressure Ulcer Risk Assessment tool which focuses on the body mass index; sex and age; level of continence; skin condition (healthy or broken); appetite; level of mobility (fully mobile to bed-bound); and, special risk factors, including medication, surgery and trauma.

- SSKIN which focuses on the **S**urfaces the person sits or lays on; regular **S**kin inspection; **K**eeping the person moving; **I**ncontinence and moisture control; and, **N**utrition and hydration.

Perform regular checks of the skin integrity identifying any problems such as blisters, breakdowns, cold areas, discolouration, hard skin, hot skin, moisture lesions, moles, pressure sores, redness, scratches, or swelling. The principle is that **frequent skin inspection leads to early detection which is then the easiest to treat**.

Regular changes to position in chairs and beds can reduce pressure on the same part of the body reducing the risk of pressure sores. The **principle of little moves more often** is good to remember. Higher risk areas for pressure sores include head, shoulders, elbows, hips, buttocks, thighs, heels, ankles and toes.

Be careful when performing move-and-handle tasks as these can result in damage to skin. For example, as a result of friction between the skin and a chair or bed.

Ensure that **skin is cleaned** properly, especially after urinary and bowel movements.

Ensure that **skin is dried** properly by dabbing dry or using a hair dryer on a cold/warm setting rather than rubbing.

Keep fingernails and toenails suitably trimmed as involuntary finger clenching can result in the fingernails digging into the palm of the hand. Long fingernails and toenails can be caught during moving and dressing.

Avoid products that dry out the skin, e.g. some soaps, body washes and talcum powder, as these can increase the risk of skin integrity issues.

Wearing the right clothing can help to protect the skin from tears.

Monitor skin after medication changes as some medications can have side effects that affect the skin, e.g. causing irritation or dryness.

Equipment:

Air mattresses can reduce the risk of pressure sores by inflating and deflating different parts of the mattress thereby mimicking the movement of a person whilst in bed. This relieves the pressure under the body by preventing parts of the body being under constant pressure for long periods of time.

Cleanliness is important and there are many **bathing aids** to help a person continue to enjoy a bath.

In the early stages of the illness there are simple devices such as **low bath seats** that help the person get their feet and legs into a better position to lift themselves out of the bath, **cushions and pillows** for comfort and support, and **grab rails** to provide increased leverage.

As the person needs further assistance to get in and out of the bath there are **inflatable cushions** and **bath lifts** which can raise and lower the person.

Other options to adapt the bathroom include switching to a **step-in bath, ceiling hoists**, etc.

Foam mattresses and **pressure cushions** can provide comfortable pressure relieving surfaces on beds and chairs that mould to the shape of the body and reduce pressure points.

Heel pads and wedges can help to reduce the pressure on the heel by evenly distributing the weight of the legs.

Incontinence care wet wipes are a gentle and hygienic way of cleaning after bowel movements.

Use and timely changing of **incontinence pads** will ensure that any urine is absorbed and removed from the skin to minimise moisture-related skin issues.

Inflatable hair wash basins can help wash hair whilst the person is lying in bed and **hair washing trays** allow the hair to be washed in a basin without the person needing to tilt their head backwards.

Soft, disposable cleansing dry wipes can be better than flannels for washing and drying.

No rinse shampoo and soap can be used to keep skin and hair clean when a shower or bed bath is not possible.

There are many **showering aids** to help a person continue to enjoy a shower.

In the early stages of the illness there are simple devices such as **shower seats** that reduce fatigue, **shower boards** and **mats** to reduce slip risks, and **grab rails** to provide increased stability and balance.

As the person needs further assistance there are **tilt-in-space shower chairs,** which may also operate as a commode. These allow a single carer to be able to perform the full shower routine including undressing, toileting, showering, drying and dressing. Many shower chairs also allow the person to be raised so that these can be performed at a safe height whilst they have various positioning options that enables the person with MSA to be put into a comfortable position, e.g. reclined, tilted, etc.

Medication and treatments:

Drink plenty of fluids and **maintain a healthy diet** as these will help keep the skin in the best possible condition.

Moisturising gloves and boots can help nourish the skin through the gradual release of moisturiser. **pH-balanced moisturisers (emollients)** also help nourish the skin.

Always **seek advice of healthcare professionals**. They can advise on how to prevent problems, e.g. using barrier creams, and how to treat problems should they occur such as antibiotics, creams, dressings, gels, lotions, ointments and steroids.

Sleep

Sleep problems are common in MSA and include rapid eye movement sleep behaviour disorder (RBD) where a person with MSA acts out their dreams. They may experience restless legs, reduced and disrupted sleep patterns, breathing issues such as sleep apnoea, circadian rhythm (internal body clock) disruption and daytime sleepiness. Problems also arise simply with how to get and stay comfortable in bed, and how care is provided to them.

Techniques:

Creating the right environment to sleep is important and this includes fresh air, the right temperature, full darkness or low levels of light and soft music.

Perform a health and safety **assessment of the sleeping area** and **remove any trip hazards** between the bed and, for example, the toilet. Consider installing grab rails to provide safe areas to hold on to.

Sleep issues for people with MSA can quickly cause **fatigue in partners** so it is important that partners also focus on their own quality and quantity of sleep.

Sleeping in a different room from the person with MSA may help the partner's quality of sleep, reducing fatigue and likely improve all aspects of care.

Ad-hoc respite care is available for partners to have a "night off" from caring and focus on their own quality and quantity of sleep.

At the appropriate time introduce **night-time care**. This usually starts with **"sleep-in" care** where the carer sleeps in the house and supports one request for care during the night. Once more care is needed the switch to **waking care** is made and the carer remains awake throughout the night providing continuous care as needed.

Equipment:

In the early stages of the illness there is equipment that helps the person with MSA remain in a normal bed. This includes:

- **Bed grab rails** to help get in and out of bed.
- **Bed rails** to minimise the risk of falling out of bed.
- **Bed risers** that can go under the bed legs at the head of the bed to create a gentle angle to help sleep. Or these can be used at both ends of the bed to raise it up to help get in and out more easily.
- **Waterproof mattress protectors** and **absorbent bed pads** to protect the sheets and mattress in the event of an incontinence issue or spilling a drink.
- **Mats on the floor** in case the person rolls out of bed to soften any fall. However, be careful that these do not create a trip risk.

- **Pillows, triangular wedge side-positioning cushion and other bed wedges** that help the person get into a comfortable sleeping position. Like many people with MSA, lying on her side became a preference for Sue and a long triangular wedge side-positioning cushion supported her back and stopped her rolling over.

- **Spare bedsheets** in case of any incontinence issues. This is especially important as the illness progresses as we found that we were constantly washing sheets so always had three spare sets available.

As the illness progresses, the person with MSA may need more advanced equipment including:

- **Two, three- or four-way profiling bed** is a bed where different sections of the bed supporting the head, back, bottom, legs, and knees can be adjusted independently. This allows the person to create a comfortable position to lie or sit in bed. Other features include anti-shear to stop the person sliding in the bed during positioning, the ability to tilt the bed at either end to help with circulation or posture, and to raise and lower the bed to help care provision and getting in and out of the bed.

- There are **many mattresses** available for profiling beds including foam and airflow mattresses to improve comfort and reduce the risk of skin pressure issues.

- An **overbed-table** can help the person and carers perform tasks and activities.

- **Slide sheets will help** in moving and handling activities. (see the "Movement: posture, bearing, balance, and strength" section for further information on slide sheets).

Other equipment that may be needed includes:

- A **buzzer** to help the person with MSA call for help during the night.

- A **CPAP (continuous positive airway pressure) machine** for treating sleep apnoea.

- **Night lights** to help reduce the risks of slips and trips during the night and assist the provision of care without the need for full lighting.

Medication and treatments:

There are **various medications** to help with different sleep issues.

Tiredness and fatigue

A person with MSA may find performing activities more tiring than normal so this section covers techniques for helping reduce tiredness and fatigue that are not covered elsewhere (e.g. in the sleep, emotion or communication sections).

Techniques:

Planning, prioritising, spacing things out and giving more time will allow energy to be conserved ahead of the activity, reduce the stress and pressure whilst doing things, and provide time afterward to recover.

Ask visitors to space out when they visit or adjust the timings of their visit, e.g. it might be better to visit in the morning rather than the evening.

Look for ways to make things easier, for example, the use of a wheelchair will conserve energy and allow the person to participate in an activity for longer.

Keep a "fatigue diary" to identify patterns or activities that cause fatigue to identify opportunities to improve things.

Review the environment to see if it may be causing fatigue, e.g. levels of lighting and heating.

Discuss fatigue, especially sudden changes in fatigue levels, with healthcare professionals to see if there is anything that may be causing it such as an infection.

Toilets and continence

The reduction in mobility can make the use of toilets more challenging. A person with MSA can also experience urinary or bowel (faecal) incontinence including both retention and leakage. These can lead to infections, anxiety and self-esteem issues. My experience is that all of this is very manageable with the right mindset of everyone involved.

Techniques:

Obtain a "Just can't wait" card. This card explains to people that you suffer from a medical condition that requires urgent access to a toilet. Not only does it help in public toilets, but many retailers will allow you to use staff toilets. These are available from different charities.

Order a Radar key. This provides access to most locked disabled toilets in the UK.

Travel with a small rucksack with toiletries. We bought a small rucksack with fresh underwear and clothes; toilet wipes and paper; absorbent bed pads (also useful for putting on seats); pads; gloves, and waste bag(s) to use when away from the home.

For women, skirts are easier than trousers, and it is better to **wear stockings or hold ups** instead of tights. This makes the process of getting onto the toilet much easier, quicker and more hygienic.

Ask the local council for **additional waste disposal** as the switch to using disposable pads and pants created a lot of household waste.

As mentioned in the skin care section, **wash and dry properly,** using a hair dryer on a warm or cold setting to help to minimise rubbing.

Watch out for **sores and broken skin** and ensure any are treated to avoid pain and infections.

Monitor bladder and bowel activity to ensure that problems are identified before they need more serious intervention. You can use a bowel opening chart and the Bristol Stool Chart to document when the bowel opened and the consistency of any stool. We paid **special attention after medication changed** as many drugs have side-effects that can affect continence.

Always strive to maintain the **privacy, dignity and comfort** of the person with MSA during toiletry activities such as pad changes. Ask visitors to leave or wait elsewhere, close the curtains, etc.

Equipment:

There are various strengths **of incontinence pads and/or pants** to help cope with increasing levels of incontinence. We started off using pads (which are available on the NHS) and then moved to pants (which are not available on the NHS).

Use fabric or disposable **mattress protectors** or **absorbent bed pads** to avoid changing the sheets if an accident happens. We also used the smaller absorbent bed pads on seats just in case there was a leakage that the incontinence pads and/or pants couldn't contain.

Place a **commode** near the bed to simplify and speed up the process of going to the toilet. These vary from fixed and folding seats to advanced powered shower/commode seats.

Consider using **toilet wipes** as these are gentler than toilet paper.

Bladder stimulators can be used to trigger normal bladder activity.

Devices to help around the toilet include grab rails, raised toilet seats, toilet seats with arm rests, toilet frames, and sticks to hold toilet paper to wipe round the back.

Medication & treatments:

Catheters can be used to help fully empty bladders.

Changes to **diet can reduce urinary and bowel issues**. The correct medication can help to **avoid constipation** and to **resolve constipation**. Increasing fibre and fluid intakes can also help minimise the risk of constipation. Medication to **slow diarrhoea** and **minimise the effects of diarrhoea** is available.

Part III

Describing MSA

There are many sources that describe MSA such as the UK MSA Trust:

> "...a neurological disorder that affects adult men and women. It is caused by degeneration or atrophy of nerve cells in several areas of the brain. This can result in problems with movement, balance and autonomic functions of the body such as bladder and blood pressure control."

Depending on whom I'm talking to, I describe MSA in three ways:

> "It is a cruel illness. It is like Parkinson's disease on speed. There is no way of slowing it down or curing it."

***

> "It stands for multiple system atrophy: <u>m</u>ultiple means many parts, the <u>s</u>ystem is the brain, and <u>a</u>trophy means wasting away. So essentially many parts of the brain are slowly degenerating which affects different parts of the body. There is no way of slowing it down or curing it."

***

"Living with MSA is like a storm.

Before the storm hits, you know something is going to happen but you're not sure what. You get subtle signs at first. A change in the wind speed, a drop in the temperature, a decrease in the air pressure, and the birds stop singing. The signs are all there, but you don't always notice them at the time or understand what they mean.

It is then that you see the clouds on the horizon. They start getting larger and darker, even potentially a yellow, green or purple haze to them. You know that something bad is coming but you hope it's not in your direction. Unfortunately, the clouds continue rolling in and then the rain hits. At first, it's small drops and then larger ones until it's a downpour – soaking you to the core.

You see lightning and then hear the thunder, worrying when the gaps get closer as you know the storm is getting nearer.

Even as the storm rages you sometimes find yourself in the eye of the storm where everything returns to an eerie calm before the intensity returns.

When the storm moves on it leaves devastation behind it."

One can view a storm, like MSA, in two different ways;

You can see it as depressing, chilling, even scary, and hide away hoping it will dissipate before it hits you.

Alternatively, you can see the storm as nature's way of replenishing and enhancing life. You can go out in the storm and enjoy the freshness of the rain on your face. You can even prepare for it and lessen the devastation.

How you see it changes the experience, which is how we approached MSA, through a positive lens no matter how bad things got.

A timeline

I was always interested in trying to understand the timeline of MSA. Most terminal illnesses are well understood and follow predictable and consistent pathways. The medical community have developed and follow generic care pathways, which give an idea of how an illness will typically progress.

However, MSA is so rare and varied that it makes it more difficult to track its development and progression. We found advice to be very broad, with statements such as "typically after about five years from first onset most people with MSA will be in a wheelchair…."

I have included a summary timeline for Sue's journey purely to show significant events, symptoms, treatments and the use of specific equipment. The timeline will be different on every MSA journey as each person is starting from a different place, e.g. their age and underlying health condition. MSA also affects each person differently so it is likely they will experience different combinations and severity of symptoms.

Trying to get ahead of the illness and being prepared for things to get worse meant that Sue was not hampered more than she needed to be by MSA, and we could live life as fully as possible.

In the table below I have included key milestones and events on Sue's particular journey and put them into five categories:

- TEST – a test performed to help with diagnosis
- DIAG – the point at which a diagnosis was made
- SYMP – the first occurrence of a specific symptom
- TREAT –first time we started a medical treatment
- EQUIP –first time we used a piece of equipment
- OTHER – other events or milestones, e.g. funding

Date	Milestone (or event)	Category
Oct '13	Multiple urinary tract infections (UTIs)	SYMP
***** summary of symptoms as of 1st Jan 2014 ***** The only visible symptom was a slight finger twitch, but she had suffered from multiple UTIs		
Jan '14	Nerve Conduction test	TEST
	Finger twitching	SYMP
Feb '14	DAT Scan test	TEST
	MRI Brain Scan	TEST
	Early onset Parkinson's disease Type 3 Severe	DIAG

<table>
<tr><th>Date</th><th>Milestone (or event)</th><th>Category</th></tr>
<tr><td colspan="3">*** summary of symptoms as of 1st Jan 2015 ***

Sue had suffered a couple of falls despite not having any walking issues such as a Parkinsonian shuffle.

She had further UTIs.

She was having restless sleep, with her arms and legs moving more than normal resulting in her feeling tired in the mornings.</td></tr>
<tr><td>Mar '15</td><td>Cardiac MIBG scan</td><td>TEST</td></tr>
<tr><td>Apr '15</td><td>Autonomic System tests</td><td>TEST</td></tr>
<tr><td>May '15</td><td>Multiple system atrophy (MSA-P)</td><td>DIAG</td></tr>
<tr><td rowspan="2">Jun '15</td><td>Personal Independent Payment (PIP) approved following submission in May '15.</td><td>OTHER</td></tr>
<tr><td>Walking stick / pole being used for stability.</td><td>EQUIP</td></tr>
<tr><td>Jul '15</td><td>Stairlift fitted.</td><td>EQUIP</td></tr>
</table>

Date	Milestone (or event)	Category
Aug '15	First carer started. We had three visits a week, each one-hour long.	CARE
	Sleep tests confirmed severe sleep apnoea and a CPAP machine was recommended.	TEST / EQUIP
Oct '15	First time used wheelchair.	EQUIP
	House adaptations started, e.g. ramps.	EQUIP
Nov '15	Social Services "Needs Assessment" performed.	OTHER
	NHS Continuing Healthcare assessment performed, and small level of funding approved.	OTHER
Dec '15	Early signs of urinary incontinence starts using pads.	TREAT
	Started sleeping in separate rooms.	OTHER

<table>
<tr><th>Date</th><th>Milestone (or event)</th><th>Category</th></tr>
<tr><td colspan="3">*** summary of symptoms as of 1st Jan 2016 ***

Sue's balance and movement were now being affected so she was walking with the assistance of a walking stick and/or me providing stability by holding her hand.

Her posture was starting to be affected with a slouch and her head was now stretching forwards and down. Her smile was now slightly drooping to one side.

Two little fingers on her left hand were clenched tight and she had lost some dexterity in her hands affecting food preparation and eating/drinking.

Her sleeping had got much worse and she was now tired a lot.

She had lost mobility affecting her ability to get into and out of the bath.

She had some mild urinary incontinence so was wearing incontinence liners.</td></tr>
<tr><td rowspan="2">Apr '16</td><td>Botox injection given for saliva.</td><td>TREAT</td></tr>
<tr><td>Wheelchair Services organised two manual wheelchairs and ordered electric wheelchair.</td><td>EQUIP</td></tr>
<tr><td>May '16</td><td>Care increased to 9 hours per day (Mon – Fri).</td><td>CARE</td></tr>
</table>

Date	Milestone (or event)	Category
Jul '16	Riser recliner chair being used.	EQUIP
Sep '16	Started sleeping in a four-way profile bed.	EQUIP
Oct '16	Mental health issues triggered by the medication.	DIAG
Dec '16	Lasting power of attorney put in place for health and wealth.	TREAT

***** summary of symptoms as of 1st Jan 2017 *****

Sue's balance and movement were now severely affected so using a wheelchair 80% of the time with the rest of the time using a walker.

Dexterity was now severely affected, and she was struggling with personal care, contact lenses and cutting nails, etc.

Starting to struggle to eat and drink. Speech getting much quieter. Unable to control saliva.

Increasing levels of urinary incontinence resulting in switch to incontinence pads.

Fragility of mental health following the medicine-induced psychotic episode. (With the help of the community psychiatric nurse Sue's mental health improved through Q1, 2017)

Date	Milestone (or event)	Category
Jun '17	RIG (PEG) fitted.	TREAT
Jun '17	Started sleeping downstairs.	TREAT
Jul '17	Serious chest infection / severe sepsis	SYMP
Aug '17	Wheelchair Accessible Vehicle	EQUIP
Dec '17	Speech down to a whisper (barely audible).	SYMP
	First time speaking to Palliative Care services.	TREAT
	Emergency medical pack delivered to the house.	TREAT

<table>
<tr><th>Date</th><th>Milestone (or event)</th><th>Category</th></tr>
<tr><td colspan="3">*** summary of symptoms as of 1st Jan 2018 ***

Sue was fully dependent on wheelchair.

Dexterity fully affected and severe dystonia.

RIG now used for all drink, food and medication. Speech pretty much non-existent.

Double incontinence resulting in switch to incontinence pants.

Increasing levels of flirtatiousness.</td></tr>
<tr><td>Mar ’18</td><td>Switch to hairdresser visiting the house.</td><td>CARE</td></tr>
<tr><td>Jun ’18</td><td>Started wearing sunglasses to reduce glare.</td><td>TREAT</td></tr>
<tr><td rowspan="2">Jul ’18</td><td>Night-time care started.</td><td>CARE</td></tr>
<tr><td>Body temperature issues due to heat.</td><td>SYMP</td></tr>
<tr><td>Sep ’18</td><td>Start of 24-hour care to cover the final two hours between 8pm and 10pm Mon-Fri and all weekend.</td><td>CARE</td></tr>
</table>

<table>
<tr><th>Date</th><th>Milestone (or event)</th><th>Category</th></tr>
<tr><td></td><td>Moved to specialist dentistry services.</td><td>TREAT</td></tr>
<tr><td>Nov ’18</td><td>First video-call appointment with consultant.</td><td>TREAT</td></tr>
<tr><td colspan="3">*** summary of symptoms as of 1st Jan 2019 ***

Sue’s main physical symptoms had not changed significantly but they had changed sufficiently that the level of care needed was now 24 hours a day.

She was increasingly more tired.

She was struggling more with vision due to glare corrected by sunglasses.

Her body temperature was fluctuating.</td></tr>
<tr><td>Jan ’19</td><td>First Botox into eyelids.</td><td>TREAT</td></tr>
<tr><td>Jun ’19</td><td>Switch to hoisting-only instead of the standing aid to assist standing.</td><td>EQUIP</td></tr>
<tr><td>Jul ’19</td><td>Used changing places rather than disabled toilets.</td><td>EQUIP</td></tr>
</table>

<table>
<tr><th>Date</th><th>Milestone (or event)</th><th>Category</th></tr>
<tr><td colspan="3">*** summary of symptoms as of 1st Jan 2020 ***

By this time Sue was bed- or chair-bound. She had limited movement in her arms, hands, legs and feet. She couldn't speak. She couldn't eat or drink. She had problems with saliva, producing too much or too little. She was doubly incontinent. She had occasional issues opening her eyelids.

HOWEVER, she was pain-free, still happy and laughing all the time, and we were still doing things and making memories.</td></tr>
<tr><td colspan="3">On the 22nd of March 2020 Sue passed away peacefully and her battle with MSA was over.

She had "beaten" MSA through her inner strength, not letting her (or my) standards drop, a drive to continue to do enjoyable activities, an amazing sense of humour, and a flirtatious interest in any young male.</td></tr>
</table>

58 appointments

(Over a six-month period from January to June 2018)

To help keep visibility and control of everything that was going on we kept a diary. It contained a list of which carers were coming when and more importantly all of Sue's appointments.

In the first six months of 2018 we had 48 appointments with healthcare professionals either at home or at hospital. To provide some insight into the different teams involved, these appointments included:

- carer team reviews (x4)
- clinical scientists (x2)
- community psychiatric nurse (x3)
- counsellor (x3)
- gastroentology (x1)
- general practitioner (x3)
- home enteral feeding team (x4)
- neurologist for Botox (x2)
- neurologist for MSA (x1)
- nutrionalist (x2)
- occupational therapist (x1)
- ophthalmologist (x2)
- physiotherapist (x12)
- podiatrist (x2)
- Specialist assessment & rehabilitation clinic (x1)
- speech and language therapists (x3)
- wheelchair services (x2)

In parallel we had a further ten appointments that kept everything running smoothly:

- bed services (x1)
- equipment training (x2)
- facial (x3)
- hairdresser (x3)
- stairlift services (x1)

As well as all the different carers (typically six different carers per 24 hours) there were the daily visits from the district nurse to do Sue's medication or sort out other issues such as PEG site infections and constipation.

Throughout these six months I carried on working in a full-time demanding job. We tried to keep our life as 'normal' as possible. We hosted six birthday parties, visited the cinema, went to a nightclub, had a week in Blackpool and bought my car.

Oh, and I should probably mention the wasps that decided to make their home in our loft and required two visits from the pest controller.

The teams and specialists

The complexity and progression of MSA is illustrated by the list of 50 specialist teams that we engaged with after the formal diagnosis of MSA (i.e. over the five years):

1. A&E consultants and teams
2. Carers – day-time - Bluebird Care & Right at Home
3. Carers – night-time – AMG Nursing
4. CCG – Clinical Commissioning Group
5. CCG – continuing healthcare coordinator
6. Clinical imaging (MRI, MIBG, CT, Ultrasound)
7. Clinical scientists (electronic assistive technologies)
8. Community nurses
9. Community psychiatric nurse
10. Community respiratory physiotherapists
11. Continence team
12. Counsellor
13. Dentistry and orthodontic specialists
14. Department of Work & Pensions (for PIP)
15. Dietician and nutritionists
16. GP doctors
17. GP nurses and advanced clinical practitioners
18. GP practice manager and community care coordinator
19. Home Enteral Feeding team
20. Local council (e.g. Blue badge team)
21. Medequip
22. MSA nurses (from UK MSA Trust)
23. Multi-Disciplinary Team (MDT)

24. Neurologist consultant – Autonomic Testing
25. Neurologist consultant – Botox Injections
26. Neurologist consultant – MSA specialist
27. Neurologist consultant – Nerve Conduction
28. Neurologist consultant – Parkinson's (our lead)
29. NHS Business Services (medical exemption)
30. NHS Clerical Services
31. NHS Commissioning Support Unit
32. Nursing teams (on hospital wards)
33. Nutricia Homeward Services – RIG feed supplier
34. Occupational therapist
35. Ophthalmology consultants
36. Optician
37. Pain Management services
38. Palliative Care consultants and services
39. Paramedics and ambulance technicians
40. Pharmacist
41. Physiotherapist
42. Police
43. Psychiatrist
44. Psychologist
45. Speech & Language therapists (SALT)
46. Sleep consultant
47. Social workers from Social Services
48. Specialist Assessment & Rehabilitation Centre
49. Urology consultant
50. Wheelchair Services

Index

Healthcare Professionals

Holidays

House Adaptations

Intimacy

Suggestions on……

Tests

Treatments

Understanding Multiple System Atrophy (MSA)

About the book

I love reading and said to Sue many times that I might write a book. As always, she was very supportive and encouraging, but I never seemed to have the time. After Sue passed away, I sat down to start writing, intending it be about the life of a CIO. It was only then I realised that our journey with MSA was much more important.

There were three main objectives I wanted to achieve by writing this book:

- to increase awareness and understanding of MSA, explain our journey and how we lived with MSA, and provide hints and tips to improve the journey for others,

- to bring into the book some of the humour we used to counter the reality of living with MSA, and

- share the wonderful relationship that I had with the amazing lady that I was so lucky to call my soulmate for 30 years.

I became motivated by a friend to finish the book before the first anniversary of Sue passing away and I'm pleased to say that I managed to do that.

About the author

I have always been an optimistic person with a passion for people. Full of energy and drive, I always look for the humour in things. These traits really helped us.

I was 47 years old when Sue was formally diagnosed with MSA and throughout our journey I supported her at the same time as doing a full-time job as the Group Chief Information Officer (CIO) at Rolls-Royce and then at International Airlines Group.

If there are any mistakes in our story, then it is all down to me. Sue had the brains, the memory and the looks. I am now a fraction of the man I was with her; I miss her terribly and think about her every minute of the day.

Printed in Great Britain
by Amazon

17897238R00169